RESCUE MEEZ

My Journey Through Siamese Rescue

Siri Zwemke

ISBN: 978-0-578-46694-1

Dedication

This book is dedicated to all of the amazing cats we had the honor of meeting. The opportunity to meet all of these cats came about thanks to a fantastic group of Siamese lovers who made all of this happen. To each and every one of you: everyone who has volunteered either officially or unofficially; everyone who has adopted; everyone who has contributed in kind or financially; every vet and every organization who has helped,

Thank You.

To the man behind the curtain, we wouldn't be here without you.

Acknowledgements

Proofreading, comments & suggestions

Aimee Ellington

Philip Gibbs

Tania Hagan

Photography

Sapphire by Dolly Berry ©2004

Preface page by Nancy Louie ©2018

Cover by Thea Mills ©2019

Koda by Amanda Thompson ©2018

All others by Siamese Cat Rescue ©2019

Table of Contents

PREFACE

I have wanted to write this book for so many years – the longer that we are involved in Rescue, the more the stories pile up, and what's here is just the tip of the iceberg. While most of the situations we found ourselves in were not funny at the time, in hindsight, knowing what we know now, I see a lot of humor in many of them and hope you will too. As I read through all of the different experiences I had, I think the most important lesson I come away with is this: no matter what you do, no matter how much you think you know, you're going to make some mistakes along the way. We are humans, after all, and that's part of our make-up. The key, of course, is to learn from your mistakes, to adjust one's behavior and actions in the future based on your previous experiences. Don't beat yourself up too much – just be sure to make improvements in your thoughts and actions the next time.

The second thing that becomes apparent is

the enormous number of amazing people that I've encountered. In our day-to-day lives we are bombarded with negativity; this tends to be amplified in the field of Animal Rescue. We grow accustomed to focusing on the bad, but when I look at Siamese Rescue in light of all the good, I'm overwhelmed with the kindness in people. Thanks to this experience, my faith in humanity has been restored.

I tried not to mention many names in the book, and I did that on purpose. There are so many people who contributed to the success of the organization, it would be impossible to acknowledge everyone. We recognize and applaud each and every one of you who helped make us who we are – there is no way we could have possibly done this without you.

While I poke a lot of fun at both myself and my mistakes in this book, I think this is a healthy thing. I come away from the Siamese Rescue experience with an incredible sense of pride at what we've accomplished over the twenty plus years of helping both cats and people. Having had the opportunity to make pawprints on this earth, having touched so many lives, both furry and otherwise, having been able to be part of such an amazing group of animal lovers – who could ask for more. I can feel confident that my time on earth has been worthwhile. I can make fun of my mistakes simply because we did emerge on the other side of them with quite an accomplishment: a healthy, non-profit animal rescue business that not only survived but improved with every experience. Siamese Cat Rescue: three thousand plus volunteers who helped place over twelve thousand cats in forever homes. A group of people who not only came together over a love of Siamese cats but who, in the process, found a family of friends. Despite all of our hiccups and faux paws, we have been pretty successful at this rescue thing.

For all of the people and all of the cats whose lives we have touched and who have touched ours, I am eternally grateful.

Siri Zwemke, CPS (Chief Pooper Scooper)

JUST WHO IS THIS CRAZY CAT LADY?

When I take a step back and reflect on my life, it's not surprising to me that I ended up in the field of Animal Rescue - after all, I spent so many of my early years trying to find someone who would rescue me. It took many years of self-analysis and therapy until I finally realized that only I could rescue myself, and now, years later, I may have finally done that. In trying to find the balance that was missing from my life, as I considered professions, I focused on fields in which I could give what I never got. It only made sense that I would end up in a career that centered around helping others. And as I soon found out, Animal Rescue is not just about the cats, but equally about the people.

If Ancestry.com were to provide one with this type of information, you would learn that I come from a long line of alcoholics – a twisted history that weaves its way through the butlers and nannies on my mother's British side, and the philosophers and high school drop-outs of my father's side. My mother expected to spend her adult life continuing in the tradition to which she had been accustomed. My father, on the other hand, was as polar opposite as he could be, in both his upbringing as well as his outlook on life. An artistic type who was gay, but could never openly admit it, he dropped out of high school, left the military, and spent the majority of his life feeling both frustrated and depressed.

My mother worked hard at racking up the debt – private schools, summer trips to Europe, dancing, figure skating, and horseback riding lessons for us. Anything and everything to keep up with the Manhattan social group she was trying to belong to. My sister was adopted at age two; I had just turned seven. I don't remember my parents ever sharing a bed; there must have been a *lot* of martinis the night I was conceived. When I was in sixth grade, the debt caught up with us, and we were evicted – leaving the Upper East Side of Manhattan in the middle of the night, like fugitives, and moving to a cabin without heat in Central New York State. There were no funds for anything but the alcohol; this quickly became the focus of my parents' lives. My world was crumbling to pieces: I ran away more than once, and for a number of years, suicide was at the top of my To Do List.

Despite having very little money, we collected animals like they were going out of style. We had horses in the pasture, stray dogs coming and going, cats that were indoor/outdoor, and chickens and ducks that also, at times, made their way into our living room. (Once we even had a hen that laid an egg on the living room couch on Easter morning.) The alcohol-fueled violence between my parents was frightening, and my sister and I were left to our own devices with respect to just about everything. Rescue has done a lot for me, not the least of which has been to help me put my life into perspective: I realized that you can end up with a lot of good, even if you started out with a lot of bad.

After making it through high school (not pregnant and never arrested, a surprise even to myself), I was determined to go to college, primarily to get away from home. My main goal in choosing a school was to find one that was close enough to feel safe, as bizarre as that may sound. All of the awful in my life had created a great deal of insecurity. At the same time, I wanted to be far enough away not to have to come home very often. I was smart but lazy, and while I sailed through high school in a marijuana-induced haze, I still managed to get straight A's. Choosing Connecticut College ("You should go to a top-notch school" said my mother, "but no, there are no funds to help you"), I majored in Asian Studies (the professors were male, liked me, and I was desperately seeking father figures), minored in Education (to fulfill my need to help others), and partied my way through college. Upon graduating, I moved to the D.C. area with my boyfriend, flitted around between jobs, and eventually discovered that legal secretaries made pretty good money – and most attorneys, at the time, were men. Several years, law firms, and lawyers later, tired of being told what to do, I launched a catering company (too many health regulations), started a tutoring service for handicapped adults (not enough income to pay my bills), then quit both of those and worked as a waitress. A couple of years later, I married Kevin, the restaurant manager - a great guy, but someone who would turn out to have very different life goals from mine. Still trying to decide what to do with my life, after watching the movie *Children of a Lesser God* one night, I decided I wanted to work with the deaf and hard-of-hearing, and enrolling at Gallaudet University the next day, went on to get my Masters in Deaf Education. My daughter, Nicole, was born right after I graduated.

Despite many unhappy years in that cabin in Central New York, when Kevin and I started house hunting, curiously enough, I found myself looking for an environment similar to that which I had known: a few acres and a house that had space for a number of animals. Unable to afford anything in the D.C. area, we bought our first home in Spotsylvania, about one-and-a-half hours south of D.C. and along the I-95 corridor. At the time, there were no jobs teaching the deaf anywhere nearby, so I took a position as director of an outdoor educational program which had, guess what, lots and lots of animals – everything from goats and calves to peacocks and pheasants.

After a few years at this job, the program folded, Kevin changed jobs, and Nicole was ready to start school. Wanting to keep her out of the public school system, we house hunted with a focus on the Central Virginia private schools. Eventually, we found a place that met the requirements of a country home with lots of room for animals (the house even came with two goats) and a good private school nearby, and we moved mid-summer.

The collection of animals had begun. Moving with us at the time were three dogs - a stray Terrier type that I had found on the side of the road, Benji, a Shepherd mix that we had showcased at an adoption event at the outdoor education center (but that was never adopted, except by me), Scout, and a Collie mix that we got from a family who couldn't keep him when they were moving, Solomon. We also had five cats – a Siamese I got when I was a teenager, named Beeky, a calico that my husband brought into the marriage, named Broadway, an orange tabby that I inherited from a family friend who passed away unexpectedly, Tuffy, a female blue point Siamese named Triscuit, and a young male blue point named Kipper. I took a part-time job at a daycare to start with; by the time the school year rolled around, I found a job in one of the local public school systems teaching emotionally disturbed children. While probably good training for some of the cat personalities I would encounter in the future, I wasn't able to handle the stress of this job for longer than two years, spending much of my time in tears. Luckily, a position as a teacher of the deaf became available two counties away, and despite requiring a commute of almost an hour in each direction, I jumped at the opportunity.

Life was pretty good, with every day packed to the gills. Kevin had switched to a job where he traveled most of the time (he kept an apartment in upstate New York where his company was headquartered), so it was up to me to cart Nicole to and from school, dance, swim lessons, play dates, and so forth. Between the commute to and from work, my functioning basically as a single mother, and the juggling of eight animals, I was just a little busy.

As if I didn't have enough on my plate, I continued to collect animals. A neighbor down the road had Jack Russell Terrier puppies, and who could resist that, so Smutty joined our family. Of course, my daughter needed a puppy for her fifth birthday, so we adopted a Lab mix, Pepper. Beeky was getting old; Kipper hadn't fulfilled the soulmate role that would be opening when Beeky was gone, so I went out and bought a female seal point kitten that we named Suki.

Ours had always been a Siamese-cat-oriented family. Before I was born, my mother (yes, because it was the thing to do) got a seal point female she named Andromeda. Every Christmas the two of them would travel to Bermuda where her stepfather ran a hotel restaurant, and the crazy cat would swim in the ocean. Andromeda was gone by the time I was born, but when I turned thirteen, it was time for my first Siamese cat experience – a male seal point that I named Ptolemy. This was not only before the philosophy of "indoor only is best for cats" was big but also at a time where there wasn't as much emphasis on the vetting of cats. While our cats were spayed and neutered, we rarely saw a vet for other reasons, despite their constantly getting into all sorts of scraps outdoors. After about two years, Ptolemy developed some very unpredictable and aggressive biting behaviors: in the blink of an eye, he would switch from a purring, lap-sitting cat to one that was viciously striking out with both teeth and claws. On more than one occasion I ended up at the doctor's office (at one point sent by the school nurse, as my mother had been too hungover to notice the bite wounds covering my arm).

We were never able to find a trigger for his aggression and certainly couldn't afford any advanced diagnostics to determine if there was, perhaps, a medical issue causing Ptolemy's aggressive behavior. Eventually, we had to have him put down. In hindsight and knowing what I know now, I was lucky he didn't have rabies; it's hard to believe my mother never suggested that we have him tested. One would think I would have soured on the breed after this experience, but not so - my next cat was also a Siamese seal point male, and he turned out to be my first soulmate cat. Beeky, short for Mozambique (Bob Dylan was a favorite at the time) was an incredible cat, and cemented my love for Siamese, despite my incredibly rocky start. He slept in my arms, kept me sane during the hissing and spitting matches my parents engaged in nightly, accompanied me to college, and then followed me to Washington, D.C., where he competed first with my boyfriend, and then with Kevin, for attention.

With the new house in Central Virginia, I tried to take the opportunity to become an "indoor only" cat family, for, by now, the movement towards cats being safest as indoor only had begun. While the other four cats bought into the staying inside thing, Kipper was holding out. In retaliation, he became my first sprayer. Used to being indoor/outdoor in our first home, he was not about to change, what with the house being situated on six tempting acres. He'd stand at the door and yowl incessantly, and if I didn't open the door within a certain time frame, he'd come find me, back up to my legs, and let loose a stream of urine all over my legs. Needless to say, indoor-only didn't last very long for Kipper.

A few months after our move we lost Beeky; he was seventeen at the time. He became the first of many to be buried in what would later become quite the animal graveyard. That was a tough loss for me – my first soulmate cat – and I really struggled with it. Not only did I feel the urge to go dig him up and bring him indoors every time it rained, but I also spent my time trying to explain to my daughter why she couldn't unearth him to see what his body looked like (she had a typical seven-year-old curiosity). At about the same time my mother, who had moved to be near us and was about ten miles away, called to say that her indoor/outdoor seal point, Dinny, had not been home for a couple of days. Dinny went out during the daytime but usually returned to the house every evening; she was afraid that he had gotten inadvertently stuck inside someone's garage or barn and couldn't get home. We made up a poster offering a reward, hanging it everywhere, went door to door canvassing the neighborhood, and notified all of the area shelters.

Not long after that, we got a call from someone who had found a seal point male matching Dinny's description. Unfortunately, it was not Dinny, but a lovely Siamese nonetheless, and of course he needed a home. Naming him Opie, he joined our crew. Opie had clearly been an indoor/outdoor cat for some time, and despite my knowing better, Opie and Kipper continued to explore the outdoors during the day, coming in at night. As can often happen with outdoor cats, and despite living in a very rural community, first Kipper, and then Opie were killed on the road when hit by a car (Opie just as we sat down to Christmas dinner) and *that* was the end of any outdoor excursions by my cats!

Dinny was eventually found, thank goodness, although that didn't stop his adventuring outside – he, too, would eventually lose his life to the great outdoors, but that was much later. Spreading the word far and wide that we were looking for a lost Siamese was what actually started the rescue ball rolling, as I would never say no when someone called about a Siamese. Pretty soon I became the area go-to person if there was a Siamese cat that needed help. Shelters started not only calling if they had a Siamese available, but Animal Control was also giving out my name to people who contacted them needing help with a Siamese cat.

Someone in Louisa County knew of a Siamese that had been left in a backyard when the family moved away, so I went to take a look. This was the county where I taught, a very poor county with a lot of indigent families. Sure enough, an overweight, very sad looking seal point male sat on the abandoned front porch, wondering what happened to his family. Well I certainly wasn't about to leave him there, so back he came to the house, and yes, you guessed it, he too joined our furry family. (By now maybe you understand why Kevin had an apartment in New York, right?) Meantime, despite already having more animals than I could successfully manage given my lifestyle, I was still searching to replace Beeky with another soulmate Siamese. I loved the ones we had, but I wanted another Beeky. None of the current crew fell into the soulmate category.

Posting a notice that I was looking for a Siamese on several animal chat boards on the internet (this was long before social media, as we now know it, existed), someone suggested I contact a woman named Erika who ran a rescue site for Abyssinian cats. Rescue? Rescue! It hadn't even occurred to me to think about looking for a rescue group focusing on Siamese, and through Erika, I was directed to a lady by the name of Charisse in Topeka, Kansas.

Charisse, a law student with an affinity for Siamese, was operating a family-run Siamese Rescue program out of her home: pulling Siamese and Siamese mixes from her local public shelter and placing them throughout Kansas. Ignoring the distance, I immediately sent her an email to find out what cats she had available for adoption. She told me the story of an eight-year-old chocolate point male named Duke: a cat that had been found in a home with the pet parakeet, both of them sitting loyally by the side of their owner who had been deceased for several weeks. The story broke my heart, and before I had even seen a picture of this cat, I decided that he just might be my next soulmate. I had to have him. I'm sure Charisse must have thought I was some crazy nut from Virginia, for what followed was a four-month email exchange between us as we tried to figure out how I could adopt Duke and bring him from Topeka, Kansas to our home in Virginia.

Meantime, back to Ming, the poor old seal point who had been abandoned on the front porch in Louisa. He would become my first clue that saving these animals was not going to come cheaply. With limited funds available and thus only able to afford the basic vet visit and vaccines, I never realized he was diabetic. I muddled through the next few weeks, trying my hardest to keep him alive. Knowing very little about advanced cat care, I spent hours trying to syringe feed him (probably the wrong type of food), puzzling at the enormous urine balls that were produced when he was eating and drinking hardly anything. Despite my best efforts, he went into what

I realized (post mortem) was diabetic shock, and we lost him. This was not only my first lesson about the hard knocks of the rescue world, but also a lesson into the costs associated with taking in cats from unknown backgrounds. In hindsight, there was no doubt I should have requested a full blood panel and urinalysis on this cat. I had so much yet to learn. Had I done more diagnostics and gotten him on insulin, I might well have been able to save his life. As that first rescue lesson, Ming was posthumously numbered VA0001.

The phone kept ringing, and the requests kept coming in. Really? In rural, Central Virginia, the shelters saw Siamese cats? I couldn't believe it, and I made the mistake of going to see the first one, and the next, and the one after that. The first and toughest tenet of Rescue to accept: you can't save them all, and if you try, you may well end up with more cats than you know what to do with. If you have ever walked into some of the public shelters, however, and have seen those sad eyes staring imploringly at you, you know how easy it is to say "yes" without giving a lot of thought to the consequences. Obviously, I had a long way to go before I would know how to make good intake decisions.

It wasn't long before my original plan to find a soulmate cat to replace Beeky morphed into way too many cats taking up residence in our home. As the number of personal animals steadily increased, things quickly started to get out of hand. I was still working full time as a teacher. Still trying to be a decent mother. And on top of that, I was juggling way too many animals, and not doing a very good job of it. I quickly realized that if I was going to continue to bring cats in, there had to be an avenue for them to go back out again. Finding the cats seemed to be quite easy, but I knew little about adoptions. My mind turned back to Charisse and all that she was accomplishing in Kansas.

I peppered both Erika and Charisse with tons and tons of questions. Always having been one to jump into something with both feet and not a lot of forethought (remember I decided to go back to school for my graduate degree one night after watching a movie), I decided that if I was going to rescue and place these Siamese, I should become official. Of course, I'd need to raise funds to support this effort, so I called the IRS and requested that the non-profit paperwork be sent to me. I discovered we needed a Board of Directors (quick, call some friends), a budget (how hard can that be), and Articles of Incorporation and By-Laws. (That's what the internet is for, right?) Within a few days, I had all the paperwork put together and submitted it back to the IRS. Twisting Charisse's arm, I convinced her that she'd like to go on this adventure with me. She was in law school full time as well as rescuing locally, so I was ever so lucky she even agreed. Charisse didn't have an internet presence yet, but Erika did, so I got back in touch with Erika, asking her if she'd be willing to host a website for us to showcase the cats we had for adoption. She reluctantly agreed, explaining that it would need to be a very static site (i.e., very few changes), as she didn't have much in the way of spare time. No problem, I thought, how many changes could we possibly need? (Um, hello... Haven't I learned anything about myself, yet?)

Next up was to check whether there were any area regulations (true, I should have done that first). I contacted the County Board of Supervisors to find out what kind of local licensing laws there were. As it turned out, there was no county designation for "rescue." I needed to apply and be approved as a "kennel" which involved a trip to the Board of Supervisors. When I approached the bench at their monthly meeting, the comment I got was "Oh yes, we have heard about you; you are the crazy cat lady wanting to save all those cats." My reputation preceded me, uh oh!

Sapphire

By now there was Sapphire, who became VA0002. A beautiful, albeit rotund blue point gal, her owner was moving to California and couldn't bring her along. The owner called saying the Richmond shelter was full, but they had given her my number, so I invited her over with the cat. We had a lovely visit – really a nice lady – and a nice cat. Blue points are typically known for being very laid back and amenable, and Sapphire certainly met that criteria. It was only after the owner left when I realized that the only impression I had given her was that Sapphire would live happily with me forever and ever. We never discussed the fact that I might actually adopt her out to someone else. The idea of getting the owner to sign a release form, allowing me to make decisions concerning Sapphire's health and placement, had never even occurred to me. Partly because I felt bad for not being clear with the owner, but also because I still wasn't set up for adoptions, Sapphire joined the family. (What's one more, right?)

By the time JoJo (VA0003) came in (a very mixed Siamese with quite a lot of white splotching), I finally started to get the word out concerning adoptions. I was advertising in the local free papers, posting pictures on the vet bulletin boards, and of course, sending poor Erika my updates. JoJo's adopter, Nancy, adopted with an agreement that she become part of my Board of Directors. Not long after this came word from the IRS that my non-profit 501c3 status had been approved, and so, Siamese Cat Rescue Center, Inc. (SCRC), with myself as the Foster in Virginia and Charisse participating as a Foster in Kansas, was official.

AND WE ARE OFF!

Meantime, thanks to Erika, the first Siamese Cat Rescue website was up and running. Overly zealous and about as eager beaver as anyone can be, I'm sure that poor Erika quickly found me quite annoying. If you know anything about computer programming, you know that continual changes to websites can't be done with a few keystrokes, and I was all about a lot of new ideas every day. Why couldn't we have rotating pictures, an area for the sales of handmade crafts, and a place to ask for donations? Surely poor Erika had nothing else to do but spend her time doing this? While she was ever so accommodating at first, it wasn't long before she realized that my continual stream of ideas and requests wasn't going to stop, and she suggested I contact a guy named Darrell who was out in Utah. Darrell and his wife were running a website known as the Siamese Internet Cat Club (SICC), a very active social group for Siamese cat lovers. Perhaps he'd be interested in hosting our website (and dealing with my continual requests for change).

Enter into the picture Darrell, aka Webmeezer, a long time Siamese cat owner who hosted the SICC site on Meezer.Org. (The name "Meezer" came from the word Siamese: S-i-a-m-e-e-z-e-r.) The Siamese Internet Cat Club, his internet baby, already boasted over 14,000 members, members in almost every country in the world. A place for Meezer worshippers to gather and post pictures and stories, this social club was a gold mine of Siamese lovers. At the helm was Darrell, with an extensive background in computer programming (at the time, working for a national gas pipeline corporation). Already busy adding to and tweaking the amazing functionality of SICC, he was eager to help by designing and developing a site for Siamese Cat Rescue. At first via email, then phone, and eventually in person, we began the conversation and website plans for SiameseRescue.Org, and shortly after that, we had a permanent internet home.

Little did Erika realize how that initial introduction would change my life in so very many ways! With the new website, Siamese Rescue was garnering interest much faster than I could ever have imagined. I definitely wasn't prepared for not only the amount of time that having the site would require, but specifically for the requests for help with Siamese cats that came in. All of a sudden, the requests weren't just local ones. I was struggling not only for money to support this endeavor but also for space to house the cats. Plus, I had jumped into this blindly, without giving any thought to any business policies and practices which needed to be set in place if I was going to succeed. And I was still trying to work a full-time job, with an hour commute in each direction.

I really struggled that first year, and for so many reasons. I had no policies in place with respect to anything: taking in cats, screening homes, adopting them out. I was saying yes to every cat that needed help, and quickly accumulating a lot of cats with long-term medical and behavioral issues that were almost impossible to find adopters for. The cats were pouring in, but instead of being adopted out, the majority were staying. By this time, we had cats in every corner of the house. While I had a very supportive husband and we both had good, full-time jobs, our finances weren't set up for the massive drain that Rescue was taking: cat food and cat litter and various other supplies was one thing, what turned into hundreds of dollars in vet bills every month was quite another. With a husband who traveled a lot, a full-time and demanding teaching position, and a small child, I was fully subscribed already, and here I was adding on a second full-time job.

Finances were the first thing to address if I was going to keep up this expensive hobby. In my spare time (hah, right?) I baked cookies and brownies, dug up garden plant extras and repotted them into six-inch pots, and duplicated the handmade children's dresses I had been sewing for my daughter. Every weekend I would spend at the local county Farmer's Market hawking my wares, and weekday evenings I set up a table at the end of our very rural driveway to try to capitalize on local traffic – kind of an adult lemonade stand. While I was ever so hopeful, no one wanted handmade children's dresses in my daughter's size, nor did they want to buy baked goods or potted plants. In a good week, if I were lucky, I'd make $20, not even enough to cover one vet visit. It quickly became clear that all the baking, sewing and digging I was doing was not going to make a dent. I needed some other ideas.

Wait! What about those 14,000 people who belonged to SICC? This was a resource just waiting to be tapped into. With Darrell's help, I started to ask for funds and support over the internet, offering up multiple avenues to donate. You could dedicate a cat-themed birthday card to someone for just $15; you could fund a cat's spay/neuter and have your name displayed by the cat's picture; you could choose to support a specific cat, and you would get a framed photograph of that cat. Lo and behold, the first donation check came in! $25 from Barbara in Connecticut, a lady who not only became one of our long-term volunteers but who also showed me that the old adage "ask and you shall receive" could be true. Maybe I wasn't going to be alone in this venture!

Once the Siamese Rescue name was out there, and of course capitalizing on the popularity of the

SICC site, the opportunities were numerous. What had begun as a whim quickly took off, gathering speed and momentum as people expressed both interest and support. Now to harness all that potential energy and put some kind of structure in place!

Meantime, however, the cats continued to accumulate; very few of them were actually leaving. Mamagayo (VA0013) was the next cat to become a permanent resident. She was a cat who was so ancient that when she came to us, the vet took one look at her and said: "This cat is older than the wind." Not more than five pounds and front-paw-declawed, she had been dropped at the Fredericksburg SPCA by her owners when they no longer wanted her. I quickly fell in love and just couldn't let her go. She was followed shortly by Whitney, a blue point thirteen-year-old, brought to us when her owners had a newborn who was deathly allergic to cats. Dropped off amidst buckets of tears (she had been a wedding present from the husband to the wife), she was such an amazingly gentle soul that Kevin wanted to keep her, and because he'd been such a good sport so far, I couldn't possibly say no. All of this despite her having urinated on him in the bed one evening, on Valentine's Day to be exact - turned out she had a urinary tract infection. Have I told you yet what a great guy he is?

Whitney was followed by Blue, a senior seal point who stayed (my daughter had become very attached to him when I housed him in her bedroom due to lack of space), Coffee (a cat from the Chesapeake shelter who came in with a reported age of five but was much closer to fifteen), and then Taraatini, (a seal point female given up when her owner had to go into a nursing home). Yes, by this point we had upwards of twelve personal cats – clearly, I still had not gotten the hang of the adoption part of Rescue.

Finances were slowly starting to sort themselves out. There was some support out there for the basics, thanks to my pleas for help on SICC. The next biggest issue was space. There were cats everywhere. What had previously been the dogs' room in our house was now where the cats were treated initially for parasites and respiratory infections when they first came in. At the other end of the house was a laundry room where I could fit one or two cats, a bathroom (plus one cat), upstairs was a guest room (plus two), my daughter's bedroom (a group), and two bathrooms (several more). When those places filled up, I invested in a number of cat playpens which were scattered around the living area, the dining area, and the kitchen. The only room my husband had insisted be totally off limits was his office downstairs.

Luckily Kevin had a job which required constant travel; as supportive as he had been, I knew he was just not that keen on the house being overrun with cats. Capitalizing on the fact many of the cats were seal points, my mother even suggested that if I named them all the same thing, perhaps he wouldn't notice how many cats we were actually housing. Before you knew it, my home had turned into Siamese Rescue Central.

We were now three months into being an official non-profit organization. Duke remained in Kansas. Remember him? He was the reason this entire thing began. Now that we had an internet presence, perhaps I could find some drivers willing to participate in a cross-country transport. For months I thought that I could drive non-stop to Topeka, pick up Duke, and turn around and come back. I would have to do this with Nicole in tow, leaving after work on Friday and returning on Sunday and, on top of that, I'd need to find someone to feed all the animals. It just didn't seem feasible. Taking a chance, I posted on the Siamese Internet Cat Club's website (quickly becoming the bulletin board where I posted all my needs), and several hundred postings and emails later, I found eight amazing individuals who offered up their time and vehicles to help this transport take place.

Charisse, whose placement options were quickly expanding thanks to the website, would drive the first leg, and since Duke was already going to be traveling in this direction, several other Siamese cats with adopters afar, would ride along. Charisse would then pass the cats along to Lisa, who lived in Kentucky - she would later become one of our long-term Fosters. From Lisa, the cats would be turned over to Brien, also in Kentucky; he would later become one of our Transport Coordinators. A fourth driver would meet Brien; they would drive into West Virginia. About three-quarters of the way, in the middle of nowhere, West Virginia, we would convene for lunch at a hotel restaurant, and I would get to meet Duke for the first time.

The transport went without a hitch. Several SICC members joined us for lunch at the hotel restaurant, taking this opportunity to put names to faces. We dubbed it the first SICC / SCRC meeting. Duke, an incredibly sweet and laid-back chocolate point, officially joined our ranks, becoming the ambassador of the very first trip of what came to be known as "The Meezer Express" Transportation System.

As time went on, Darrell worked wonders with the website. Developing what came to be known as MOMS, or the Meezer Online Management System, his opus to the Rescue, he was able to program together such a fantastic system that truly boggled the mind with both its versatility and specificity to our needs. Eventually, MOMS would cover every volunteer function: the intake/evaluation and adoption of cats, the screening of the applicants, the various fundraising avenues offered, and, of course, the Meezer Express Transport System.

The Meezer Express grew into one of the most impressive "branches" of our organization if you will. At one point, we had nearly 900 volunteer drivers headed up by eight Transport Coordinators. The scheduled trips, which took place each weekend, were so well coordinated and detailed it was not to be believed. Over the years, the Transporters logged over 2.5 million miles. Having such a great system in place and so many wonderful volunteer Transporters allowed us to move, during our busiest years, up to seventy-five cats in any given month from foster home to adoptive home.

With Meezer Express, the adopters had a much a wider range of choices, since they could choose a cat that was up to ten hours away. Once a cat had been chosen by an adopter based on pictures, videos, and phone conversations, a Transport Coordinator would design the trip. They would take into account the three to eight cats that would travel at one time, figure in all the different starting points (as they typically came from different foster homes) and look at the various ending points (all were going to different adopters). They would set meeting spots (Cracker Barrels were a favorite as they offered the opportunity to have a quick breakfast if you got to the pickup point early); each leg of the trip averaged about an hour and a half. They would then send out requests for help to the transport volunteers in our database who lived anywhere near the route being traveled.

Once available drivers were found, a detailed itinerary was developed. The itinerary not only specified which cats were on what leg, but what kind of car (make, color and license plate) was being used for each leg of the trip. In the early days, it would often take over a hundred emails back and forth to coordinate each trip; as Darrell programmed more and more capabilities into the MOMS system, much of it became automated, and a trip itinerary could be generated with a few keystrokes and a look at Google maps.

On the day of the trip, the Fosters of the cats involved would pack the cats up in a regulation-sized carrier which the adopter had purchased. The carrier would have a small disposable litterbox inside as well as a food and a water dish clipped to the door. A label would be printed with the Foster's name and information, cat's name and information, and adopter's name and information, and would be attached to the carrier. The take-home bag (also known as the "goodie bag") would be readied. This would include everything from the cat's medical records and required health certificate, to their bed, food, scratcher, and favorite toys. The first Transporter would arrive at the foster home at the crack of dawn, loading up the cat(s) and goodie bag(s). From here, it worked like a relay system, only it was the passing of cats, not a baton. (Oh, and no racing allowed.) At the designated meeting point, the driver would hand off the cat and goodie bag to the next Transporter. Cats would join or leave the trip at certain points, depending on where their final destination was. As each driver completed their leg of the trip, they would check in via email or text to update the status of the transport and to report on how the cats were doing on the trip. The adopter would usually drive the last leg, and the final Transporter would have the pleasure of turning over the cat and goodie bag to the new owner.

Of course, there were many hiccups in the beginning before Darrell had formatted the system - we certainly made mistakes. There was the adopter in Illinois who called to say that the Transporter had never shown up with her cat and no one could find the driver. It turned out the driver had fallen in love with the cat and, not realizing it had been adopted by someone, taken it home. *Lesson One: Add a clause to the Transport Rules stating that the cats are the property of Siamese Rescue and the drivers may not deviate from the trip as planned.* There was the Transporter who was to meet the next driver at a rest stop in New Jersey at midnight, and the second driver never showed up. *Lesson Two: Require that all drivers have a cell phone and verify, through a screening process, they are reliable.* There was the cat who, just before transfer to his new adopter, had such a poo explosion that the entire back seat of the car was covered. *Lesson Three: Require that all Transporters have a transport kit that includes paper towels, wipes, clean pads, and sanitizer.* And one of the best ones: the time that the police chief in Kentucky called to let us know they had one of our Transporters in a holding cell because of the number of unpaid speeding tickets she had, and asked us what we would like for them to do with the cats that were in her car. *Lesson Four: Add a question to the Volunteer Application about outstanding tickets.* (The police chief finally let her go, with the cats, when he heard about the purpose of her trip.)

Early on in Rescue, for very long distances, we

were even able to provide some air transportation, as we had two volunteers whose husbands were airline employees. Because of this, the volunteers were occasionally able to fly the cats, space permitting. These trips also had their hiccups, and eventually, we stopped flying any cats, but there were definitely some memorable flights. There was another poo episode, where there was so much of an explosion that it coated every inch of the airline toilet, to the extent the flight attendant had to place an "Out of Order" sign on the toilet. There was the cat who freaked out at the security checkpoint and managed to escape her collar and run wildly through the airport, only to be tackled by the foster mom who dove behind a Welcome Desk to grab her. There was the flight attendant who was asked to hold the cat carrier for a few minutes while the Transporter shifted seats, only to have the front of her uniform soaked in cat pee when the cat decided to urinate through the soft-sided carrier. And then there was the Transporter who was bitten so severely going through security that both she and the cat were covered in blood, the EMT's were called, and somehow, despite all this commotion, the Transporter managed to convince them to let her board the plane with a crazy cat in tow.

Duke's maiden journey was coordinated without the fancy MOMS system that was developed later on and was uneventful. While future transport regulations required all cats stay in the carrier, and all carriers be seat-belted in, Duke traveled on the front seat of the car, not in a cat carrier.

Duke

GOT YOUR PASSPORT?

Once we had an internet presence, the breadth of coverage we could achieve was truly impressive. What started with the first few volunteers willing to help Duke quickly morphed into a group of Siamese lovers who were very supportive of our efforts in every way possible. It wasn't long before I no longer needed to spend Saturdays at the Farmer's Market or to stand at the end of the driveway hoping someone would stop and buy cookies. I found that just by getting the word out and asking for support, people were very generous, and the Siamese Internet Cat Club was a fantastic resource for finding help in so many ways. SICC quickly became my go-to place: an amazing community of people who helped with everything from supplies for the cats, to funds for their medical work, to the ever pressing need to grow our volunteer base.

Meantime, however, space continued to be a serious issue; there was never enough room to find spots for all of the cats that needed help. I still didn't know how to say no when someone asked. It was a Monday morning when the local shelter called, begging us to take this tiny blue point Siamese named Squirrel who had been turned in by her owner. As what is termed an "Owner Give-up," she was on their euthanasia list and only had a few days left. (Strays were held by the shelter a set amount of days in case the owner is looking for them; owner-turn-ins often didn't have the luxury of a hold period. If space were tight, they would be the first to go.) Her owner had said she was friendly in the home, but at the shelter, she was absolutely terrified, not eating and cowering behind her litterbox. Of course I had to take her.

Her arrival at our house coincided with yet another bout of upper respiratory infections. The ex-dog room (which was now the cat room) was full of sneezing kitties, and every other available room and cat playpen was full. Kevin had just left for another stint at the office in New York, with a firm admonition *not* to put *any* cats in his office. That door was to stay closed and the room was off limits. Kapeesh?

With nowhere to put Squirrel except for the carrier she came in, I was at a loss as to what to do. I knew from my little bit of experience that Owner Give-ups were often terribly stressed when placed in a cage because they had never experienced cage life before. The owner had reported that her eating and litterbox habits were perfect, and the Shelter Director felt that if she could just get out of the cage and into a small room in a home, her friendly personality would reappear. Now I happen to have a very Pollyanna-type personality, and I was sure that the Shelter Director was right – given a few days in a quiet room, she'd revert back to the cat she had been in the home and be fine. It was early in the week; Kevin wouldn't be home until Friday. What he didn't know wouldn't hurt him, right? Of course, I'd have to take certain precautions, but that wouldn't be hard.

I started by securing everything in his office, removing any knickknacks that might get knocked over. I cleared off any desk clutter, carefully placing the items in a box in the order that I had found them, knowing that I would need to recreate the same scenario. I set up a carton on the floor for Squirrel to hide in, along with a teepee tent and a covered litterbox. My plan was to have her in the office for a few days, and by the time Friday rolled around, I'd have an opening in my daughter's room and could move Squirrel there, as the two cats in that room were being picked up by their adopter on Friday morning.

All was well for the first twenty-four hours. While Squirrel certainly didn't improve by leaps and bounds, she was hunkered down in her bed, was using her litterbox, and was eating and drinking. I checked on her before I left for work the next morning and she was fine. When I got home about eleven hours later, however, she had vanished.

Now I've had cats hide before, and seek hard enough and ye shall find. But this cat was nowhere. Squirrel was gone to the point that after seriously looking in every possible space imaginable in the office, the only thing I could come up with was that she had somehow managed to get out of the room. Could it be that my daughter had let her out, and was afraid to tell me? Or had I unknowingly let her slip through my feet as I entered and exited the room? I really didn't think either of those options were possible. However, I still searched the entire house just in case. There was no Squirrel anywhere.

My feeling of panic started to rise. Leave food out, and she'll show herself eventually, my newfound friends on the internet told me, but it was the word "eventually" that had me a little panicked. I readied a smorgasbord of every type of temptation I could think of, but by then it was Thursday morning, and the food remained untouched. The realization was setting in that within thirty-six hours, the office would need to be occupied by someone else, and there was no doubt that person was going to be one unhappy camper. It was time to get really serious. I knew deep down she just could not have gotten out of the room, so inch by inch, piece by piece, I started dismantling the office.

The file cabinet came apart. The bookcase was removed, everything was taken off the shelves. Any and all boxes were opened, the contents double and triple-checked. One by one, I removed them from the room. Keeping an eye open as I carted things out of the office, I was sure that I would see a grey streak go flying by, but no such luck. Gradually I got everything cleared out of the room except for the desk: a large piece of oak furniture that Kevin had brought with him into the marriage. In the middle, a pencil drawer, which opened and was partially empty. On each side, file drawers, easily opened, nothing but files in them – but just to be sure, I removed all the files. On the top of the file drawers, on each side, a drawer, not more than four inches high. Left side – drawer pulled opened – there was a stapler, some stamps, various odds and ends. Right side – huh – it was locked. Then I remembered. This was where all the important pieces of life were kept – you know, the passports, the car titles, the marriage license – the type of things that perhaps (no, definitely, as it turned out) should be kept in a safe deposit box. But, hey, it was a locked drawer, and they should be safe in the drawer, right?

Except that when I pulled the desk away from the wall, I found, to my horror, a three-inch slit in the back of the desk that accessed the drawers from behind. Now seriously, and I'm not exaggerating, we're talking a tiny slit that could allow entry if you were a large mouse, or perhaps a gerbil, to an only slightly larger four-inch high drawer. A drawer that was locked. And sure enough, when I stuck my fingers into that slit just to see what I could feel, yup, you guessed it, I felt fur. Nope, not just fur in the back of the desk, but fur inside the four-inch area that was the locked drawer. The drawer that had all those essential papers in it.

So now began the search for the key. I had no idea where that could be. I looked everywhere I could think of, but there was no key to be found. And *no*, I was *not* calling Kevin to ask him where the key was because, gulp, I just couldn't share the reason I needed to get into that drawer. Of course, it would have been way easier at this point in time if I owned up to the imminent disaster because, by the time he did come home two days later, the entire drawer had been crowbarred apart to retrieve one very smushed cat. (She was in way better shape than I was.) And all those important papers? Why there were all ruined – for yes, she had peed in fright while I was dismantling the desk. While I succeeded in taking the desk apart, there was no way to put it back together, and, yup, you guessed it, my goose was cooked.

When I tell you later that Kevin and I get divorced, you won't be surprised, right?

Squirrel

If this experience didn't make it clear that I really, really, had too many cats in the house, I don't know what would. My numbers weren't helped by the fact that our address was now out there on the website, and even before the popularity of GPS, people could still easily find us. Oftentimes we would wake up on a Sunday morning to a family of four strolling through the garden, waiting for the doors of the Center to be unlocked, or to a pick-up truck with a crate of kittens sitting in our driveway when we got home from the grocery store. Once we even came back from an outing to find a Siamese cat that had been left in a crate on our doorstep in the heat of the summer. Changing the wording on the website to indicate that we were open by appointment only and that we didn't accept drop-offs helped a little, but there were still plenty of occasions when people would just show up at all hours of the day. Once, a family even showed up on Christmas Day, thinking they would bring their kids to play with the cats.

It was a Sunday afternoon in May; we were sitting outside enjoying our front deck when someone drove up in a great big black Cadillac – tinted windows and all. Unable to imagine who we knew that would be arriving in such a car, I walked over to see if I could help. An enormous man got out of the car, asking if this was Siamese Rescue. When I said it was, he stated that he needed to rehome his two Siamese cats. His new wife would not let him in the house with the cats, and he was absolutely stuck as to what to do. Peering through the tinted windows, I saw no sign of any cats in either the front or the back seat. I explained that we did not take in cats on the spot and that additionally, we currently had no space available for any more cats. If he could go home and get pictures of the cats, I suggested, and then send those along with any medical records to me, I promised him we would see if we could find some space as soon as possible.

Mr. Cadillac Man sadly shook his head. That's not going to work, he explained. He had been turned out of his house, along with the cats, and was not allowed to return home until the cats were gone. When he saw my puzzled look as I peered yet again inside the car, he moved to the back of the Cadillac, motioning me to follow him. Popping open the trunk, there, hunkered down, were two seal points, looking fairly terrified, huge wide eyes staring up at me. No crates, no blanket, nothing, just two Siamese in the trunk of this big ol' Cadillac. And then, Mr. Cadillac Man's eyes filled with tears as he told me how much he loved these boys, but his new wife had laid down the law in no uncertain terms. He had driven three hours to find us, and he just couldn't go home with the cats still in the car.

So once again, despite not having any space, two more cats joined our program. (Fortunately, they turned out to be absolutely wonderful cats and as a bonded pair, placed very quickly.)

As you can see, it was not only the fact that I did not yet know how to say no, but the fact that I kept getting myself backed into these corners (sounds like a good excuse, I'm thinking). Turning to SICC once again, I poured my heart out to the members, lamenting how I had bitten off so much more than I could chew.

One of the people who responded was a lovely lady from Texas named Tonja who ran her own consulting company, and as a result, had all sorts of financial connections. What started with a lot of emails, and then progressed to long phone chats, ended up with Tonja flying out here in person to get to know me and the needs of the organization. Suitably impressed, Tonja stepped up as our primary fundraiser, not only helping to spread the word far and wide but also persuading many of her business contacts to financially support our fledgling organization.

Convinced she could raise whatever funds were needed, Tonja and I concocted a plan to put another building on our personal property to house the cats. We had an area, not a hundred feet from the house with an old goat shed, and it would be a perfect location for a second structure. Kevin and I thought this to be an absolutely great idea, for as it was, our home was filled each weekend with strangers in every room of the house visiting with the different cats. Poor Kevin, he was traveling every week, week after week, for business. He'd get home on Friday nights after an incredibly stressful week, wanting to do nothing but relax. At home, he would find that there was not one moment of privacy. The steady stream of visitors, using our bathroom, laying on the floor in our bedroom reaching under the bed to pet a scared kitty, arriving at all hours of the day and evening, many times without notice, was taking its toll on both of us. And the cats kept pouring in – what had started as a whim, was quickly taking over our lives. A separate building to house the Rescue paid for by donated funds sounded like a fantastic idea.

Finding a local architect, we had plans drawn up for what would look like a two-story garage on the outside (for property resale purposes), but inside the building would house cats instead of cars. The downstairs would house the cats who had finished their quarantine time in what we would come to call "Group Living", and would be filled with cat furniture of all types. There would also be a sink for dish washing as well as a bathroom/laundry room. Upstairs would be three separate areas - an "Isolation Room" for the new cats, a "Step Down Area" for the cats cleared of quarantine but not quite ready to integrate, and the office/lunch room, where the scaredy cats could hang out. The building would be set apart from the house with a separate entrance and a small parking area for visitors. After meeting with a local attorney to make sure we had all of our bases covered, we started moving forward with building the Rescue Center on our property.

Fast forward about three months. Tonja had done an excellent job of fundraising, and while we didn't have all the money in hand, we were close. It was at this point that someone suggested I look into getting some grants. One of our volunteers had some experience in this area, and together we took on researching, writing and submitting grant proposals to many different places. We were eventually awarded funding, not only to help finish building the Center but to furnish it with commercial cage banks and other needed supplies.

It was at this time that the "Millie Bed" project started. Originally called Tammi beds (she introduced the pattern to us), later overseen by a lady named Millie and then by Pat, this cottage industry, in which several hundred Crafting Volunteers participated, became our number one fundraiser – year after year after productive year. Not only the most popular item sold in our online retail store, the beds were also the one item that customers clamored for at the different cat shows attended by our Events Team. The beds, and later on the pads, snugglesacks and craft items made a significant contribution to our yearly income.

Shortly after the shelter was built, we went to file our yearly IRS paperwork with the help of our local accountant. Surprise, surprise. Did you know that you cannot use funds donated to a non-profit to build something on personal property? Obviously the local attorney didn't, but it makes sense, right? Unfortunately, we were learning the hard way. Realizing that in order to comply with IRS requirements, we had to buy back the building from the Siamese Rescue Corporation with our own funds, plus interest, was quite a shock. This would now make it the most expensive garage in the neighborhood.

Oh well, it's only money. What's a little more debt. Despite that major hiccup, and thanks in large part to Tonja, we now had an official Center for the cats.

Meantime, back at the ranch (which, seriously, she called it), Tonja was so in love with our mission that she decided she too wanted to get involved in rescuing Siamese, with a focus on the Dallas Fort Worth area. Turning her expensive home into Siamese Rescue Texas, she joined our ranks. Initially thinking we could all be one big corporation with individual state chapters (Virginia, Kansas, and now Texas), we quickly discovered this to be way more difficult than we thought. County rules were different, state reporting requirements varied, and the IRS paperwork became a nightmare.

Additionally, we all had different philosophies on how a joint organization should operate. In the end, we opted for three separately-funded and maintained organizations, all sharing website space. Poor Darrell had taken on a bit more than he bargained for. Thus became Siamese Rescue Central: the Mother Ship in Virginia, with sister organizations in Kansas and Texas. We would be joined later on by Colorado, Northern California and Southern California: separate organizations sharing website space and ultimately resulting in over 25,000 cats saved.

Talk about dynamic: changes and growth were happening so quickly, one could barely keep up. The Center was not only completed but well furnished. By this time the media had gotten wind of us, thanks to several volunteers who worked to share the word. All of a sudden we were on *Fox News*, *ABC News*, written up in *Cat Fancy*, mentioned in *Better Homes and Gardens*, and featured on the television show *Virginia Currents*. It was all great publicity, with the end result being that things got even busier. Volunteers, donors, and adopters were starting to ante up, and Meezer Domination was beginning.

THE MEEZER GODS ARE WATCHING

By now you may have figured out that I tend to go a bit overboard when I get focused on something. If I were to count all the cats I've personally adopted over the years, the number is a staggering forty-three. (A little side note – I am also pretty allergic to them, but if you love something enough, it's worth all those Kleenex.) The personal adoptions were not only because I fell in love with some of the cats we met and couldn't bear to adopt them out, but more so because, early on, there were so many medically or behaviorally compromised elderly cats that we just couldn't find homes for, so we kept them. I might only have them for a year or two, but I really enjoyed getting to know so many wonderful geezers (as we called them). The benefits of living with so many great purrsonalities outweighed the fact that we might only have each one for a short period of time. It goes without saying that with so many cats passing through our lives as personal adoptions, eventually I would find not just one, but two different cats that filled the hole Beeky had left behind. But Rescue did more than just help me find the right feline to adore!

My first husband, Kevin, is a wonderful man, the father of my daughter, and someone I will always hold very close in my heart. After fifteen years of marriage, however, the life tracks we were following only had us traveling further apart. He was climbing the corporate ladder and very successful at it; in doing so, he needed to be in the vicinity of whatever large corporation he was currently involved with. Such corporations were unlikely to be found in rural Virginia, plus we were miles from a decent airport. I was following my dream of country living, on a six-acre spread of land with lots of animals. As we both became deeply entrenched in our individual lives, and as Rescue started to blossom into a real business and not just a hobby on the side, it became more and more apparent that our life paths were no longer converging, and we amicably agreed to divorce.

Despite it being the best decision for both of us, the timing couldn't have been worse for me. Even though Kevin traveled a great deal of the time, having someone, even part-time, to help with all that was involved in home ownership and raising a small child was better than doing it alone. My life was so overflowing at this point, I was literally struggling to keep my eyes open. I would wake up at 4am to feed twelve personal cats, five dogs, and twenty-some rescue cats, then get my young daughter up and ready for school. More often than not, I would drive twenty minutes in one direction to the vet office, leaving whatever cats were scheduled to be seen that day in the airlock, details taped to each carrier, as their office was not yet open. Next was thirty minutes of backtracking to drop Nicole off at before-school daycare; from there it was forty-five minutes to the school where I taught the deaf. I had students in two different schools (elementary and high school), so would rush back and forth between the two schools, trying to provide coverage to both (the county could only swing one of me). After teaching all day, I would repeat the drive, only in reverse, picking up Nicole who had gone to after-school daycare, then picking up the cats at the vet. If we were lucky, we'd get home around 6pm. Then there would be thirty to forty furry mouths to care for, followed by getting dinner for both humans and supervising homework for Nicole. About 10pm I'd sit down at the computer for several hours of emailing, answering queries and then brainstorming, with Darrell, new ideas for the Rescue and the website. I remember in those early days laying my head on the pillow about midnight every night and immediately falling asleep, thinking I could not have fit one more iota of anything into my day.

It wasn't long until my daytime teaching job started to suffer. At one point I even fell asleep while driving on the way home from work. Luckily, I was at a traffic light, so I woke up when a car behind me pulled up and honked. However, it was the day that my principal found me collapsed in the classroom, tears running down my face, that it became clear something had to give. She drove me to the local doctor, waiting with me while I was seen. Diagnosed with exhaustion, I was sent home. That was the day I realized I could no longer teach and run the Rescue at the same time. It was either the kids or the cats. At the end of that year, I made the official career change, giving notice at my teaching job and taking on Siamese Rescue as a fulltime endeavor.

Darrell, who was still in Utah, was experiencing similar marital differences, and he and his wife also parted ways amicably. The more time Darrell and I spent together on the phone and over the internet, the more we realized how much we had in common. It wasn't too long after Darrell divorced that he packed his bags and moved to Virginia. Fortunately, he was able to transfer to the Charlottesville office of the company he was with, about a forty-five-minute commute.

At the time, Darrell and his wife owned seven cats, but there was a lot of feline discord in the home. It was decided that his wife would keep the four cats that were tightly bonded. Darrell would keep his seal point girl, Britainy, and we'd work to assimilate her with the residents here. The other two male seal points (the troublemakers of the group) would come to Virginia, but we would rehome them through the Rescue program. For years, they had been tormenting the other cats, causing a lot of urination issues in the home. We knew that adding them to my twelve was not going to work. On the first of several trips here, the boys flew with him in cabin. We logged them into the Rescue program, and they were adopted out very quickly by a lovely lady in Connecticut with no other cats. Darrell, of course, stayed in close touch to see how they did, and it was very reassuring to hear how they blossomed (and stopped spraying) when they were the only two cats in the home.

Britainy, his seal point girl, was to stay in the family, and she traveled with Darrell on a second flight a few weeks later. A confident, outgoing seal point personality, Brit was having none of the "in cabin under the seat in the cloth carrier" business, and from the start of the flight, made it known that not only was she on board, but she was not going to be a great traveler. If you have ever heard a Siamese female at full yowl, you can imagine what that flight was like. Darrell had to quickly remove himself, and Brit, to the airport lavatory where Brit proceeded to first chew through the cloth carrier, then to shred Darrell's arms as she ricocheted off the tiny bathroom walls, leaving streaks of blood all over everything. While at first the flight attendant demanded he take a seat, when she peeked in and saw Darrell's white polo shirt covered with blood, she quickly agreed that spending the rest of the trip in the lavatory with Brit might be the best choice for all concerned.

It seemed that all of Darrell's trips from Utah to

Virginia were fraught with adventure. Perhaps this gave him a clue as to what was to come. On another visit to Virginia, I decided to combine picking him up at the airport with a trip to the Fairfax County shelter. The Fairfax shelter had been dealing with a hoarding case in a well-to-do neighborhood – over 120 cats had been found in a woman's home, some of them deceased, many of them ill. The situation had been brought to the attention of Animal Control when the neighbors started complaining about the smell emanating from the house. As it turned out, the majority of the cats were Siamese, and not yet having any kind of intake screening in place, we agreed to take sixty-eight of those cats sight unseen. On this particular trip to get Darrell, I was stopping first at the shelter to pick up ten of the unneutered males to bring back to the Rescue.

It was July, and Virginia hot and humid. The pick up of the cats went without a hitch – I had told them I was on a tight timeline as I had to get to the airport, and they had the cats ready to go in carriers. This was just as well, for if I had seen how semi-feral some of them were, I might have thought twice. Arriving at Dulles for a 1:30pm pick up of Darrell, I found his flight from Salt Lake City had been delayed. Delayed, not just by a few minutes or half an hour, but by three hours.

Have you ever been closed in a car for three hours with a bunch of Tomcats? In 100-degree weather no less? Even with running the air conditioning every so often, you can't even begin to imagine the odor that quickly permeated everything. (Did I tell you my car had that nice new car smell up until this event?) The smell of that car was never quite the same after that experience.

About a year later, Darrell and I tied the knot – and the merger of SICC and Siamese Rescue was official. Our wedding was held at the Center under the guise of a fundraiser for Siamese Rescue, open invite. Despite having one heck of a time finding someone to officiate at the wedding (turns out rural churches are not all that accommodating if you're not a member or have been divorced), we were married by our Postmaster. Who would have thought Rescue would have allowed me to find not only furry soulmates but a human one too.

This finding of one's soulmate on the internet, over a common love of Siamese, was not the only time I questioned whether there were Meezer Gods at work. A lot of things fell into place for me to meet Darrell. One could argue that growing a relationship over several years, via telephone and internet, laid a solid basis for a great marriage. However, this next "coincidence" really made me wonder about the powers that be.

Before my mother met my father, she dated a man by the name of Howard. While they chose not to marry for whatever reason, their friendship continued even after my mother married my dad. My mother was working as a professional photographer at the time, and Howard was very involved in both photography and painting. During the early years as I was growing up, Howard was the family friend who joined us for bike rides through Central Park, treated us to meals at his favorite restaurant haunts, and joined us on many family outings. When a money issue raised its ugly head (I suspect my parents had borrowed money from Howard that they couldn't repay) and my parents stopped talking to him, he and I remained close. Even after my family was evicted from our Manhattan apartment and moved to the cabin in Central New York, Howard would often pay for my train ticket down to N.Y.C. to visit him for the weekend. He'd put me up with one of his female friends, take me to a show on Broadway, escort me out to eat at his favorite restaurants, and we'd end the weekend with a visit to his art studio to review and discuss his latest oil paintings. Throughout what were very troubled years for me as a teenager, Howard was the primary person who kept me grounded. When my life was falling apart, and I was thinking of ways to escape, he encouraged me to hang in there. He was convinced I was destined to have an impact on a lot of lives.

Howard came to my college graduation, met and critiqued my boyfriends, and danced at my first wedding. When he was hospitalized with stage four lung cancer at fifty-five (never having smoked a day in his life), I was devastated and traveled to N.Y.C. to be by his side. He left me with a huge hole in my heart, his camera equipment, and his cat, Tuffy, a lovely orange and white Domestic Shorthair with one kidney, who lived out his life with us, passing away five years later on the actual anniversary of Howard's death. That was coincidence number one.

Fast forward eight years to my first year of Siamese Rescue. There's a young cat I was fostering that found a home out on Long Island. Meezer Express was still in its infancy, and we were trying to figure out how to get this kitty from me in Central Virginia to this family in New York. As I was discussing the possibilities with them on the phone, they mentioned that they had a son in college in Richmond, VA, named Josh. He would be traveling up the I-95 corridor in a few weeks, and could possibly bring the cat along if I could meet him at a rest stop on I-95. Only forty-five minutes from me, this was very doable, and given his name and number, I called him directly to iron out the details. Introducing myself, we made a plan to meet at McDonalds on the following Saturday at a preset time. Two days before our meeting, I got a call back from Josh, who said he had something off the wall to ask me. "You didn't by any chance ever know a guy named Howard who lived in N.Y.C., did you?"

Turns out that Josh was best friends with another guy, whose parents were close friends with Howard. As the story went, when Howard's apartment was boxed up after his death, the son of Howard's friends somehow ended up with a manila envelope with my name on it. It had been passed along to Josh a couple of years before when he was headed to college in Virginia as they knew I, too, was somewhere in Virginia, but trying to track me down had never risen to the top of the priority list. For several years, this manila envelope had been in a file cabinet in Josh's home and seeing my name, Siri, not the most common of names, had triggered his search for the envelope. Now, here he was, transporting a cat to his mother from a Rescue that I started.

It got even stranger. We met at the McDonalds and traded the cat for the envelope. I was sitting in my car, by myself, staring at this manila envelope, almost afraid of what I was going to find. Finally, I slit it open. Inside was a packet of pictures. Every photograph was of myself with various animals – cats, dogs, ducks in the park, you name it. Now Howard took thousands of photos over the years, and of many subjects besides animals and me. On the back of one of the pictures, in Howard's handwriting, was scrawled – "your love of animals will be your strength." How cool was that? Was it a message that he believed in what I was doing, or maybe even somehow had a hand in it? I certainly like to think so!

WHAT COMES IN, SHOULD GO OUT

One of the most common questions we get asked is “How can there possibly be so many Siamese out there that need rescuing?” As is true of almost any breed of animal, if you look hard enough, and in enough places, you will find plenty of them. It doesn’t matter if the breed is Maine Coon, Persian, or Dalmatian – you just have to get the word out to enough people, and cover enough territory, and before you know it there is a long line of animals, from every awful circumstance you can imagine, that need help. This can lead to one of the biggest mistakes that private rescue groups can make: not understanding the laws of supply and demand. If we were going to adopt out cats, which was one of our primary goals as a rescue, then we needed to bring in the type of cats that people wanted to adopt. While it would be nice to think that we could save them all, and while it can absolutely be said that all animals deserve a chance, the reality is that there is always likely to be more need for help than there is space with any one particular rescue group. Of all the cats out there, some of them are not going to be adoptable. They may have never been socialized to humans. They may have long-term ingrained behaviors that can't be changed, whether from neglect or abuse. Or they may have terminal illnesses that may not be short-term and may be very expensive to manage. So while it may be hard to turn down cats that need rescue, if, as a small rescue group, one intakes too many cats that have issues which no one wants to take on, then one quickly fills up all of the space available with cats that aren't going anywhere.

Here lies an important differentiation for our purposes – a rescue versus a sanctuary. A sanctuary, defined as a place of refuge or safety, is a long-term living environment for animals that need it. These are often animals that do not have many other options. While some animals at sanctuaries get adopted, many live out their lives in this environment. Ideally, the sanctuary has ample space: the animals may live in large groups indoors or outdoors; if they are adoptable and can find adopters, that's great, but if not, they live for as long as they have in a safe, healthy and controlled environment. The input of animals is always greater than the output. As such, sanctuaries often have large numbers of animals.

A rescue, for our purposes, is more like an

adoption agency. Our goal is not just to rescue animals, but to be able to rehome them to an environment where they can be successful. To do this, one must intake animals that have the potential to be adopted.

The mistake we have seen many rescue groups make is that instead of saying "No, we have no space," they work to fit just one more animal in, figuring that every animal deserves a chance. While that is, without a doubt true, in order to house animals in a safe and healthy way, space is eventually going to be limited. The more animals that share space, the more health and behavior concerns that can crop up. If one doesn't make good intake decisions, little by little, more animals come into the rescue environment, more issues arise, and fewer and fewer animals leave. Before you know it, you've got a situation with way too many animals and way too few adoptions. The amount of elbow grease and finances required to maintain them properly is often not available, disease and behavior issues can become rampant, and eventually, the entire effort can collapse.

There were quite a few times when we were asked to help a well-meaning person who had rescued a lot of animals, but then found themselves well over their head. Whether it was a landlord who was threatening to evict them, finances that were collapsing, or simply that they were overwhelmed, it was always a challenge to step in quickly and scoop up a lot of cats from a would-be rescuer. Without the structure in place: first and foremost, the finances to care for the animals, secondly, the space to house the animals in a healthy manner (both physically and emotionally), thirdly, the time and manpower to care for the animals, and finally, the policies and procedures to guide the entire process, it is easy to cross into a crisis-type situation.

Of all the lessons that Rescue has taught me, this was probably one of the more difficult ones to learn. Ask anyone who has looked into the eyes of a sad or frightened animal – or an animal in a situation that clearly is not a great one – it is very difficult to turn away. Ideally, a Rescue is able to do much more than physically intaking cats from awful situations. They might network with other groups and individuals who may be able to help; they might provide mentoring and support services to improve the environment in the hopes that the animal may be able to stay in the home; they might market the animals that the organization personally can't help. The key is to find alternative solutions because there just isn't the space to intake them all.

Fifteen years into running the program, we were able to intake the more difficult cats - the diabetic cat, the fifteen-year-old, or the cat with cancer – for by that time we had developed a following of adopters who were willing to be the repeat caretakers for this type of hospice cat. At first, however, without this base group of "Geezer Guardians," as we called them, we didn't have a clue how to choose good adoption candidates, and we found ourselves not only with way too many cats in way too small a space but with many cats that were not adoptable. Just look at how many of those early intakes ended up staying in our house. We could easily have crossed the line from rescue to cat hoarder if we hadn't had the determination to make this not just a Rescue, but a successful non-profit business.

I still had quite a ways to go, however.

It was sometime in late May; the weather in Virginia was typical in that we were getting quite a bit of rain. I got a request from the local shelter to help a lady in the western part of our rural county (way up in the Shenandoah Mountains) whose husband had called in, threatening to set fire to a trailer filled with cats. Apparently, there were six Siamese housed on the property; all the shelter could tell me was that her husband was more than fed up with the situation. Six cats didn't sound all that overwhelming, so I agreed to drive out there one afternoon with carriers and take the cats. (Big mistake – don't agree to something when you don't have the entire story.) What a great adventure to go on, I thought. This was an opportunity to show off my rescue skills to my mother, who had been ever so subtly questioning the use of my graduate degree to scoop litterboxes. Packing up the carriers, my sixty-eight-year-old mother and ten-year-old daughter in tow, we headed up into the hills of Madison County.

So there we were: a car full of carriers, me dressed

in shorts, a tank top, and flip flops, my mother and daughter similarly dressed, as if we were out for a picnic. A drive through the most rural parts of the mountains of Virginia (no four-wheel drive vehicle) on what basically turned out to be akin to a goat path, with deep muddy crevices in the road. Who knew that Madison County extended so far up into the mountains? The road became narrower, ruttier, and more difficult to traverse. Eventually, we arrived at what appeared to be a single-wide, very rustic looking trailer. Behind that, we could see several decrepit buildings that were clearly uninhabitable. It was mid-afternoon, a high of ninety degrees and humid, and a car so full of naivety you could cut it with a knife. Greeting us as we arrived were a bunch of chickens and guineas running everywhere, several goats whose ribs were clearly apparent, and four mangy looking dogs lunging from their chains in a very unwelcoming manner. My efforts at exuding confidence for my mother's and daughter's sake were rapidly diminishing!

As we parked, out came a surly looking bearded man, corncob pipe dangling from his lips, rifle grasped in his hand. Determined to be the heroine here, I exited the car, holding a cat carrier in front of me (all the time wondering whether a cat carrier could actually deflect a bullet). In a Virginia dialect I couldn't make heads or tails of, he rattled off something I probably needed to know, spittle flying from his lips. Pointing in the direction of several collapsing buildings down the lane, he parked himself on the stoop, rifle across his knees, and proceeded to stare sternly at my mother and daughter.

Turning back to the car, I suggested they stay put (no worries there, they were both looking a bit ashen). Skirting the snarling dogs and hoping their chains were strong ones, I headed over to what appeared to have once been a shed of some sort. The building was half sunk into the ground and falling in on itself; the roof dipped like an upside down umbrella. Old wooden stairs on the side were splintered through, and the one broken window was boarded over. The door was stuck, and as I forced my way into a room about half the size of a one car garage, a stench like none I had ever known hit me in the face. The floor was ankle-deep in feces, urine, and very small skeletons of who knows what. (Really? And I wore flip flops? What the heck was I thinking?)

The cats (supposedly six, but impossible to count) flew by at the speed of light, launching themselves in fright, fury, and desperation from wall to ceiling to wall. Across the floor, up one wall, back across the ceiling and down again. The only thought that crossed my mind was the scene in the *Wizard of Oz* where those monkeys were flying towards Dorothy!

At least I could see that they were actually Siamese. There were four seals and two blues, and while they appeared to be quite unsocialized, they didn't look to be in horrendous shape. There was an enormous bag of cat food torn open on the floor, a bowl of extremely filthy water, and absolutely nothing that you could call a litterbox.

After about thirty minutes of chasing each cat, any cat, with a carrier, I was close to tears. I was so unprepared it wasn't even funny – I had no gloves or blanket, let alone any kind of catch pole – and definitely no experience with this type of scenario. There was no way I was going to get my hands on any of the cats; they were just too frightened. The best I could hope was that I could corner each of them and somehow herd each one into a carrier, but I was having no luck. Retreating to find my corncob pipe smoking buddy, I managed to borrow a tired-looking throw blanket from him. Returning to the shed, I set carriers in various positions around the room, wedging them against the walls, pushing them down into the ankle-deep feces, hoping they'd stay lodged in place. I started waving the blanket at the cats, trying to herd them towards the carriers. Maybe, if I were lucky, they would understand that the carriers were their tickets to freedom. I was finally able to blanket one of them – a pregnant-looking blue point who obviously didn't feel that well - and got her into the first carrier. Another forty minutes later, after doing the dance of the bullfighter, a second, and then a third, ran into the carriers. Figuring I should leave while I was ahead, I managed to exit the building, and property, with three cats who now ricocheted within the confines of their carriers, a mother who was clearly wondering whether I had lost my mind, and a daughter who was rapidly developing an aversion to Rescue.

What happened to the rest of the cats? I explained to Animal Control what I had found and what I was able to do and apologized profusely that I couldn't help any more than I had. Of the three I brought into Rescue, one was a seal male (Shammy) who was placed with a wonderful lady with the patience of a saint. While it took some years, he went on to develop into a lovely cat, thanks to her dedicated work. The second one, Chicory, also got placed. Unfortunately, he never socialized very well, but he was able to live out his life with a family of humans and cat buddies. The blue point, Nikko, had a very tough time of it. Sure enough, she was pregnant, but the fetuses were deceased, and that caused quite advanced complications, so she stayed with us for quite some time while she recovered. Once she felt better, she became much more social, and she went on to be placed with a lovely young lady as her first cat ever. Had I learned my lesson? Not yet – it was still several more years before I learned not to commit to anything sight unseen.

It wasn't long after this that Darrell joined me for another adventure in catching a flying Siamese. With the death of an elderly owner and an estate to be settled, the executor, who herself was well into her nineties, called us one day to ask if we could please come to get this cat that was left in a townhouse which was being readied for sale. No, she didn't have any information on the cat; no, she didn't know if the cat was eating, but she thought so; and no, she hadn't even seen the cat but knew it was in the house somewhere. Oh, and by the way, the cat came with a nice sized portion of the estate to whoever would take her. Perfect timing, as we were still raising funds to get the last bit of the Center completed. Off Darrell and I went to a lovely neighborhood in Alexandria, with row townhouses that were quaint, expensive, and sinisterly dark inside.

Meeting us at the door, the executor let us in and then took her leave. "The cat must go," she said, "Goodwill is coming this week to clear out the house." Carrier in hand, we explored the three levels in the townhome to no avail; there was no sign of any living creature anywhere. We found a bowl of cat food that the neighbor had been filling, and some signs that food had been disappearing, so we knew Mariah was in the house somewhere. Room by room, bit by bit, we started searching: looking behind curtains, pulling out furniture, crawling over and around belongings, hoping we would find a Siamese. Finally, on the second floor in one of the bedrooms, there she was, and there she went, a flash of dark barreling up the stairway, heading into the farthest reaches of the master bedroom and into a very dark and extremely cluttered closet. At least she looked to be a Siamese from what we could see!

There's nothing like digging through the contents of someone's personal boudoir that you don't know, and even more so, is now deceased. It was plain spooky. Slowly, we removed item after item from the bedroom, dragging it out into the hall, and what we couldn't remove, we moved to the corner. We then took everything out from the closet, working on getting close to what turned out to be a hissing, spitting bundle of fur – without a tail! As it turned out, the tail had been chopped off at some point when the cat got in the way of the stair lift mounted on the steps. After a lot of crashing and banging as we tried to corner her and get her into the carrier, and with just a wee bit of blood, (ours, not hers, for we had not thought to bring any gloves), we managed to get the poor cat into the carrier and brought her back to the Center.

Poor Mariah was *so* angry by the time we got home that we gave her the spare bedroom upstairs in the house. We figured that she'd be happier there and wouldn't get what we term "cage rage," something seen particularly in cats given up by their owners when they are put into a cage for the first time. In our experience, stray cats are, more often than not, okay with the cage experience, for they are delighted to have shelter, food, and water, Owner Give-ups, however, can be very put out. They can display some real aggression and violent behavior if they don't have much cage experience in their past, making it very difficult to work with them. At least in the bedroom, she would have a homey environment, one which would hopefully help her calm down and become more pleasant – and ideally, of course, adoptable.

A week passed, and no such luck. Mariah was

still one angry and upset cat. She was rushing at me - lunging and spitting every time I opened the door. There was no way I was going to get close enough to handle her. I would walk into the room with my daughter's soccer shin pads on, long falconry gloves and cookie sheets in my hands to ward off any attacks. She just wasn't calming down. Blocking off access to things she could get under, we were finally able to get her into the corner where we had left the original cat carrier. With the bullfighting blanket trick, we herded her back into the cat carrier. Here she crouched, eyes big, round and dark, growling and hissing, daring me to get close.

The biggest worry during this entire time was her lack of food intake. Despite putting down the same brand of food she had been fed in her previous home, she was so upset that she was showing no interest in eating. Now cats are not like dogs. Dogs, when hungry enough, will eat just about anything, but cats can be stubborn as can be, and once their stomach starts getting that nauseous feeling from not eating, they slowly begin to shut down. After not eating for some time, the body starts moving stored fat to the liver to be converted into energy. Unfortunately, cats' livers are not set up to deal with large quantities of fat, and a cat's health can quickly go into crisis mode if they go too long without food. Clearly, Mariah needed some syringe feeding to keep her going, but with those long claws and sharp teeth, there was no way I could get a syringe anywhere near that mouth. By this point, it had been close to a week, and I knew I needed to get some food into her or we were going to lose her. We had to come up with some sort of plan.

So we got resourceful. Armed with a bowl of AD (a high-calorie food supplement sold by the vets and jokingly called Almost Dead by many), a turkey baster, and a long piece of aquarium tubing, we came up with a system. With Mariah in the carrier, I was able to close the door with a long pair of tongs. I then tipped it up on end, with the front door facing the ceiling. I filled the turkey baster with AD, stuck the end of the baster into the aquarium tubing, and snaked the tubing into the carrier, aiming at Mariah's face. Ready and squeeze! AD (a beige goopy mess) went everywhere – all over the carrier, which was fine, but also all over her face and body. While very little appeared to end up in her mouth, to my delight, she was so perturbed at being covered in the stuff that she started cleaning herself like crazy. To hear her grumbling while licking herself was hilarious. At least she was getting a bit of nourishment!

One of the good things with syringe feeding (or in Mariah's case, baster feeding) is that it often doesn't take much to prime the pump, so to speak. Once a cat gets enough food in them to get over the nauseous feeling that comes from having an empty stomach, they will often show more interest in food. While Mariah still wasn't eating much on her own, she was starting to feel a bit better about life. From that point forward, when I entered the room, she knew what was coming. After the first time or two, she would actually get into the carrier on her own and wait while I positioned myself, filled the baster, and coated her in AD.

A few weeks later I took advantage of her being in the carrier and carted her to the vet – time to finally get her checked out and her vaccines updated. At the vet, while by no means super friendly, the white coat must have scared her into submission, for she could be handled. By this time, our vet was familiar with our Rescue – she knew that the cats I brought to her would already have been looked over carefully, treated for mites and fleas as needed, and would come with a list of any issues noted that I wanted her to check out.

With Mariah, however, I got a very curious look from the vet when I came to pick her up. “I understand that you might not have been able to clip nails on this gal,” said the vet, “but what I can’t figure out is why in the world her ears were absolutely filled with beige goop." We both had a good laugh as I explained my technique of syringing the AD via a turkey baster!

Not long after this, we were visited by a true Mother Teresa of an adopter – a mom of several adopted children who worked for social services in North Carolina. Having seen Mariah on our website, she drove all the way from North Carolina to Virginia specifically to adopt her. Ignoring my warning that she might never come around to be a friendly cat, this adopter was dead set on taking Mariah. "She needs a home," she stated, "and that's that." She had one of her special needs adopted children with her when she visited, a boy who clearly had a connection with animals. They both spent quite a bit of time not only with Mariah but also visiting the other cats we had at the time. One of the others, a scrawny chocolate point named Sweet Lamb, really took a shining to this boy, and he to her. While Mariah was the one they had come to adopt and the one that they left with, it was not an hour after they left that she pulled back into our driveway to adopt Sweet Lamb as well. "Sweet Lamb needs a home just as much," she said. An amazing adopter – this was what Rescue was all about. This warm fuzzy feeling, doing something not only for the cats that needed a new home but in this instance for a special boy who needed a new friend, was what made everything worthwhile. We came to call this type of feeling the paycheck of Rescue.

WORMING MY WAY OUT OF RINGWORM

Another referral that came in was from a nearby Culpeper cat rescue group – they were full up and was there any way that we could help? An elderly lady had called them; her son felt she had way too many animals and said that he was going to drown her cats if she didn't get rid of them immediately. Most of them, they said, were Siamese. Not fifteen miles from me in downtown Culpeper, on a small side street of row houses, these cats were reportedly already caged, so I felt much more confident this time around. Tossing a few cat carriers in the car, I went to see if I could help.

The house, although tiny, was fairly normal looking from the outside – and yes, we know looks can be deceiving. At least it wasn't falling down on itself or anything. But sure enough, once inside the front door, the situation was quite alarming. The living room was packed, wall to ceiling - cage upon stacked cage of not only cats but dogs of various sizes and birds of different kinds. In the middle sat a toothless woman in a recliner, surrounded by all those crates. I could clearly see why the son was making a fuss (and in all honesty, was surprised the neighbors weren't complaining). It was not only loud, but smelly and dirty. However, the animals did at least look to be both bright-eyed and friendly. The Siamese cats and they were Siamese, (yay!) ranged in age from small kittens to young adults. Every animal was eager for attention, and paws of all sorts reached through the cage bars towards me. Pulling some of the cats out, they were easy to handle, friendly and outgoing, and ever so anxious to escape their situation. While feeling a little sick to my stomach at having to leave the dogs and birds in the house, I eagerly accepted all eight of the Siamese, confident that I could find homes for them quite easily.

Arriving home with several more cats than I had originally planned for, I once again faced the question as to where to put them. This was before the Center was built, and every room in the house was packed with cats. There were two old male Siamese in my daughter's room, a sneezy female in the guest room; a pair of young adult chocolate points in the laundry room, and a lynx point female with her kitten in Kevin's office (after the Squirrel incident, he finally gave in to the Siamese invasion). I then remembered that I had recently seen an ad in the free weekly paper for a set of metal chicken coops that a local farmer was getting rid of. Depositing the eight cats in our bedroom temporarily, I sped off to collect the coop cages. Several trips back and forth and I managed to get them set up in the dogs' room. They were small (each coop cage not much larger than a very large cat carrier) but workable, they stacked, and while it wasn't a big improvement on the situation that these cats had come from, I knew it was only temporary while I worked to get some of my other tenants adopted. Once again, I was making the mistake of too many cats in too small a space and not enough elbow grease (let alone funds) to go around – particularly given that at this time I was still working full time at a "real" job.

The first treat was to find that these cats were infested with both ear mites and fleas. So eager had I been to help the little furry faces looking up at me that I didn't look closely at their condition, and while I tackled the ear mites with ear cleanser, Q tips, and ear drops, the fleas were another thing altogether. Fleas are great jumpers, and it wasn't long before the entire household, my daughter and self-included, were itching from flea bites. Flea baths are nice but somewhat ineffective in getting rid of the live fleas. It takes either the topical or systemic meds to be effective long-term, and at eight dollars a pop, well, I was trying to conserve funds. And, of course, with fleas (and with any type of unhygienic living situation) comes both roundworms and tapeworms – lovely wiggly things that can be quite stomach-turning. Fortunately, these critters are easily and quickly treatable, although, after all was said and done, I did end up having to flea bomb the entire house.

Two weeks passed. I had been able to find the funds to treat everyone with topical flea medication, and I was feeling pretty good about all the nasties I had eradicated. Now that the eight cats were almost ready for adoption, it was time to move them out of the coop cages and into the rest of the house. Since several of them were younger, and all seemed very cat-friendly, I divided them up and integrated them with the other cats I had sequestered in the various rooms.

One thing I couldn't understand, however, was the little bits of hair loss I noted here and there. At first, it was just a spot on one of them, then on another. They were small spots, mostly on their faces, particularly the younger ones, but here and there on the paws as well. (Some of you know where this is going, don't you?) Thinking they may have had a reaction to the fleas, the flea medications I used, or the shampoo I washed them with, I didn't worry too much at first. However, not two weeks later, what had started as just a few spots here and there was rapidly spreading over their stomachs and legs. I remained puzzled, the mystery deepening about ten days later when I noticed that these round, hairless spots were showing up on the other cats as well. I was so focused on trying various ointments and salves to stem the spread of whatever this was, it took me a while to notice that I too was breaking out in dime-sized circular red patches all over my torso. And lo and behold, they soon showed up on my daughter as well. (By this time, it was becoming clear that Nicole was highly unlikely to choose Rescue as her career path.)

Clearly, this was becoming one of those times where a vet visit just could not be avoided. Better late than never, I know, but funds were so tight I had really been hoping to treat this on my own. (I was a little late in discovering that trying to do so was going to be such a *big* mistake.) Packing up the now twelve cats affected, off to the vet we went. To my horror, my principal's horror, my daughter's teacher's horror (and don't forget Kevin, you can imagine how he felt), we had our first experience with ringworm.

Now if you're a seasoned rescuer reading this, you're nodding your head, probably with a bit of a grin on your face. You know that ringworm is a fact of Rescue unless you're lucky enough to live in the northern third of the U.S where it's cool enough that it's rarely seen. It happens, it's the pits, but it's fairly common. We treat it, we clean up after it, and we move on. For a newbie, however, I was in high panic mode. What do you mean my daughter can't return to school, and all of her classmates' parents need to be notified? Are you serious that I can't be in the classroom teaching until this has cleared up? Still so brand new at this Rescue thing, I made some of my most embarrassing phone calls ever: to other area rescue groups. After introducing myself and sharing my predicament, I had the audacity to ask them if they would *please* take these ringworm cats off my hands. I'm sure they all had a huge laugh after hanging up the phone, completely amused at my inexperience and naivety!

If you're familiar with ringworm, you know that it's not a worm at all, but a fungus that spreads like crazy and loves all species. It can go from your cat to your dog to you to your horse and back again. Here in Virginia, it's quite commonly found in the soil; if not careful, one can even bring it in from the garden (yes, I did that too one year). An outbreak can be the bane of elementary school systems, quickly becoming an epidemic if you're not careful. While one would hope careful isolation and cleaning would keep it contained, when you're dealing with something that can travel on the tiniest bit of litter, be tracked on your shoes, and swoosh through your air vents, it can be a nightmare. One cat with a little bit of ringworm is one thing, but twelve cats in all parts of the house is quite another. And even once those cats are adopted out, ringworm can live on in your carpets and rugs for a very long time. Well, we had wanted to get rid of all the carpeting in the house anyway, what better opportunity than this. Once again, this was all getting a bit more expensive than I had envisioned.

Eventually, I was allowed back to work, my daughter was allowed back in school, and all those cats went home. It took a lot of fungal baths, a lot of medication, a lot of laundry, and a great deal of time. Oh, and of course, quite a bit of money.

Goodness knows how many households I may have unknowingly infected with ringworm. Back in the early days, we sent cats home to adopters without nearly as much after-the-fact information and assurances as we were able to provide later on. And hey, I got all new laminate flooring out of the deal. Suffice it to say after this experience, when we visited a cat in the public shelter to determine if we were able to accept it and it had ringworm, we thought carefully before taking it on. And one of the first modifications we found we needed to make to the Center after it was built? Separate air handling for the Isolation Room!

It wasn't long after my first ringworm experience that the Animal Shelter called again – this time they had a Siamese cat that had been turned in as a stray, and yes, she was friendly. Did she have any skin lesions I asked? A cat already in a cage *and* friendly to boot. And no lesions noted. I had covered all my bases; how could one go wrong?

If the ringworm experience had taught me one thing, it was to invest in some good fungal shampoo and to have an intake protocol of not only examining the cat but whenever possible, immediately upon entry into the home, bathing the cat. The old dog room, filled with metal chicken coops, was now officially converted into my cat examination and bathing area. While bathing isn't a hundred percent effective solution against ringworm, it does allow one not only to see the cat's coat and skin condition (more easily viewable when wet), but also to remove any contaminants on the fur. Ringworm spores, invisible to the naked eye, can be found on many cats that have either been outside or have been living in awful conditions. The spores have to migrate to skin level to actually cause an issue with a particular cat, although many cats won't actually show lesions if their immune system is strong enough. That doesn't help, however, the other cats, people or dogs being exposed to the cat that is carrying spores on their fur. Therefore, getting those spores off is always a good idea before integrating the cat into any household.

Over the years, that entry bath also became my number one way to assess a cat's personality. While one would think that all cats hate baths, the reality is that by doing it upon entry to a new environment - during a time when the cat is typically already traumatized by a car trip and change of situation - you can tell a great deal about what the cat's base personality is like. Some cats, believe it or not, sit and enjoy the bath, and will even purr. The cat that behaves like this is a childproof cat, a cat who, despite whatever wild toddler they are presented with, is likely to be just fine. Other cats, when being bathed, will try to bite at every opportunity. This is the type of cat that when faced with the wrong circumstances, (again, let's think about that wild toddler) is likely to nip. In a rescue situation, where the goal is to adopt the cat out as quickly as possible to make room for the next cat coming in, identifying these types of personality traits as early as possible is extremely helpful. Even the smell that comes off the cat provides you with valuable information – did they come from a house full of smokers? You can smell that in their fur. Were they kept in a garage, or found hiding under a car hood? Sometimes you can smell engine oil. Did the woman in the home douse herself with perfume? These tidbits of information become apparent when the cat gets wet. Because so many of the shelter cats came to us with no history whatsoever, the more clues we could gather early on, the better matchmaking we could do when finding an adoptive home.

Off I went to the local animal shelter to visit the friendly stray cat with no lesions. Home came Sheena who had been found as a stray, and who, as I had learned to expect by now, was covered in fleas. She was a lovely chocolate point snowshoe (meaning, for our purposes, she had white paws), with a really friendly and laid-back personality. She was somewhat round in the stomach: maybe pregnant, I thought, but worms will also do that, so I wasn't too worried. I set my vet visit for Monday morning: spay, exam, and vaccines.

Siamese Rescue's goals include both a decrease in the unwanted pet population as well as a quick turnaround from intake to placement. This way we can maximize the number of cats we help. While some readers will disagree with the spaying of a cat known to be pregnant, the reality of tiny kittens in Rescue is usually not a great one. For one thing, the mother is often unvaccinated, or, if they went through a shelter, they might have been vaccinated while pregnant. This can affect the kittens developmentally. The mothers typically did not have decent prenatal nutrition or care, as they were often outside as strays. Finally, whenever you have teeny tiny kittens in a rescue environment, it is close to impossible to keep them from being exposed to the viruses, bacteria, and parasites (oh, and don't forget ringworm) that is looping through the air vents. The toll that it takes on the foster parents, who give it their all to try to pull some of these compromised tiny kittens through, only to lose them, is awful. Therefore, if the vet felt it was still safe for the mother, and the pregnancy was still in the early stages, we would spay the cat.

Back to Sheena. Time to get down to work with my new intake procedure of a fungal bath. There was no way I was going to let ringworm get the upper hand this time around. Sheena was very cooperative for the bath, which was nice since I was so new at bathing cats. Once she was wet, however, I was quite alarmed at just how large her stomach actually was. Huh. I guess she was pregnant after all. And not just a little pregnant. Well, we'd see what the vet would say on Monday when we went.

I had just started congratulating myself on my proficiency with bathing when Sheena began with some very plaintiff mewings. Now realize I have no experience with pregnant cats, and it never occurred to me the possible implications of a warm water bath on a quite pregnant cat. (When I had Nicole, the doctor never mentioned a bath, he told me to have a beer.) Sheena was squirming around and looking quite uncomfortable, so I quickly washed the rest of the shampoo off and removed her from the laundry sink. Wrapping her in towels, I started rubbing her down, when the meows, and the squiggling, became a bit more frantic and higher pitched. Plopping her quickly into a large dog crate I had readied, she started some circling behaviors, pawing at the towels. Uh oh. This didn't look to me like litterbox behavior. Sure enough, around and around she went, until she plopped over on one side, the mewing continuing. And then not one, not two, but over the next few hours, six small Siamese kittens made their appearance.

While I wish I could say I had fond memories of raising my first-ever litter of kittens, that was not the case. Sheena was still covered with fleas, even though she had just had a bath. You can't treat newborn kittens with any flea medication, nor can you safely bathe them, and shortly after birth, those kittens were also infested with fleas. Consequently, I spent hours and hours with tweezers trying to pick the fleas off the six tiny kittens.

A few days later, Sheena came down with an upper respiratory infection. This could have been from the stress of change, the fact that she had not been vaccinated, or because I bathed her. This meant that all the kittens got sniffly, and kittens have trouble nursing when they can't breathe, so it was touch and go for a long time with several of them. Between cleaning off their noses, trying to get them to nurse, and picking off the fleas, there was little time for anything else. And yes, despite my very best efforts, ringworm raised its ugly face yet again. The only good news was this time I was able to contain it within one room, for I had moved that dog crate into a spare bedroom so that Sheena could have some privacy. While there was no doubt there were days when it was good fun, particularly as the kittens got older and bounced around as kittens will do, it wasn't without an enormous amount of work. On top of that, I couldn't help thinking about how many other cats I could have helped during those ten weeks they not only took up one of the bedrooms, but most of my spare time.

Sheena

Eventually, all six kittens went on to be successfully adopted, as did Sheena, but it wasn't without a great deal of effort and angst. That experience was probably the reason that throughout the years of Rescue, I always let the Fosters be the ones to take on the kittens, for I felt that all of the trouble that kittens brought with them made them just plain evil creatures (said in the fondest of voices).

DON'T BITE THE HAND THAT FEEDS YOU

By now you may be thinking that I'm a slow learner, given that I kept ending up in precarious situations with cats who were, to say the least, a little tricky to manage. Mama Thompson was yet another one of those. (Hang in there, I'm getting better.)

Naïve, maybe, but always thinking about the poor cat, it didn't occur to me that driving an hour to an unknown location in the middle of nowhere, in response to a phone call from a strange man, could be considered somewhat risky. I was more focused on the cat he had trapped (yes, the key word here is t-r-a-p-p-e-d) that had been living under his deck for some time and was continuously producing kittens. Getting her off the streets, spayed, and into a rescue program where she could be adopted was my focus. When I let Darrell know what I was doing (he was still living in Utah at this time), he insisted on staying on the phone with me as I went to meet "Joe." At least one of us was thinking, although I was not sure what he'd actually be able to do from out there should something go awry – I'd be long dead and buried by the time he found me.

With my phone connection to Salt Lake City in place, I arrived at Joe's home, swinging my carrier, ready once again to be the heroine and save yet another cat. Fortunately, I was not met with a rifle this time. Considering some of my home visits to date, Joe seemed quite normal. Taking me out back, he pointed me towards a trap sitting on his back deck. Inside I could see a somewhat fat looking tortie point cat that was eyeing me suspiciously. Once again, (I know, I know) it didn't occur to me to question whether the cat was adoptable or not, and I asked him to remove the cat from the trap and place her in the carrier. While I didn't think my request was a crazy one, Joe certainly did. Looking at me with a "you have got to be kidding me" expression, he handed me the cat, trap and all. Having taken him months and months to catch her, there was no way he was going to open that trap door. I would have to take her as is, he explained, and I could return the trap at a later point in time. (If I had been listening, I suspect that Darrell was making some wise-ass comments at this point, but he was tucked safely in my pocket, so whatever he was saying fell on corduroy pants.) Would I ever learn to just say no?

By this point, at least, I knew that I should go directly to the vet for spay and vaccines, as it might be hard to catch her again (this, by the way, was a real understatement). Calling the vet's office, I explained the situation and told them that I was on my way. Being in a rural area, they were quite experienced with feral cats, and they managed, without too much trouble, to get her out of the trap, vaccinating and spaying her. While still sleepy from the anesthesia, they transferred her into a cat carrier for me. I suspect that there was quite some discussion behind my back as to whether I knew what I was doing or not, thinking I'd be able to find an adopter for this cat!

Once I got back to the Center, it was time to transfer her from the carrier to a playpen. It was at this point that I realized just how feral she actually was. Did you know that feral cats can walk on the ceiling? Well, I should have known, as I'd had previous experience with my flying monkeys. This cat exited the carrier at full speed; there was no way in hell she was going to go into a playpen. Loose in the downstairs of the Center was the best that was happening, and so Mama Thompson, as she came to be known, disappeared into this very large room full of cat furniture, where she spent the next few weeks incognito.

Fortunately, she had a good appetite. I would see her each day, hiding behind or underneath something, and would place her food nearby where she could easily access it. Unlike some of the other frightened kitties we had taken in, other than some eye contact, there was very little forward progress. This was not a cat who had, at some point, been someone's pet and then gotten outside, but more likely a cat who had been born outdoors and had no experience with indoor living. While she would follow my movements with her eyes, there was no slow blinking, as cats will do when they show you some trust. She was ready to flee anytime anyone got too close. Well, she was vetted, and so for the time being, she could just live as the untouchable cat in the Center, not a big deal.

Now, remember that we designed the Center as a two-car garage in case we ever needed to sell the property in the future. (There's probably a limited market for purchasers of a country home with a cat shelter attached.) We had covered the garage door openings with thick, sturdy chicken wire so that when we raised the doors in the warm weather, the cats couldn't escape. Spring in Virginia is just glorious, and there were many days that we would take advantage of the fresh air, the doors open wide and the cats lounging on the tile floor warmed by the sun. They loved it, and we loved being able to bring the outdoors in (although after the fact, we realized we also brought in lizards, fleas, and even the dreaded ringworm).

It was one such busy Saturday with volunteers and adopters visiting; the garage doors were wide open to the beautiful weather. I was giving a tour of the property – starting with the recently built Center, and then moving over to the house to show everyone what we called the Geezer Ward (our bedroom) where the twelve resident cats hung out. The day wore on, and as it cooled down, I excused myself to return to the Center to close the garage doors before the cats became chilled. Pressing the garage door button from the inside, I heard chalkboard nails accompanying the rumbling of the overhead door as it rapidly descended to the floor. To my horror, I realized - a little too late - that there was a cat perched on top of the garage door, riding a rollercoaster towards the great outdoors. Too late to stop the doors, I raced outside, thinking I could catch whatever cat it was as they slid down the door. Who was it, but Mama Thompson, sailing towards freedom – except that, as the garage door straightened into place, her toenails got caught in the crack of the door fold. There she was, hanging by her toes on the outside of the door.

I'm not sure who was more alarmed, her or me, but focusing only on the fact that I needed to grab this cat before we lost her to the outdoors, the ramifications of putting my hands on a truly feral cat never crossed my mind. I grabbed her scruff with my left hand, using my right hand to lift her body weight while I tried to maneuver her toenails out of the door crack. Obviously scared to pieces, she closed her mouth around my right wrist, chomping down tightly. Dropping her scruff with my left, I switched hands and attempted to scruff with my right, holding her up with my left hand. With great agility, as only a cat can, she flipped over and closed her teeth on my left wrist. At this point, in quite a lot of pain, I let go with both hands, the only good news was that Mama Thompson had now freed herself from the door. I was left standing there with blood streaming down both of my wrists, trying very hard not to faint. Meantime, Mama Thompson was heading for the hills at full speed. "Help, help" I managed in not much more than a whisper. Staggering into the Center, blood dripping everywhere, I wrapped my wrists in towels and stumbled back to the group of merrymakers in the house. "Excuse me, but could someone please take me to the hospital?"

I recovered from that episode thanks to antibiotics, pain killers, and a visit from Darrell who flew out from Salt Lake City to see how I was doing. And Mama Thompson? She was nowhere to be found, despite setting traps, posting notices, and notifying the local shelters. Since we live in a very rural setting and there are plenty of outdoor cats around, I wasn't too worried, but certainly felt bad, as if I had somehow failed her. All that trouble and effort and now she was lost. At least I knew that, at a minimum, she had the experience to navigate the outdoors, and in all likelihood, she was no worse off than she had been when she was previously over in Joe's neighborhood. Plus this time she was spayed, so we didn't need to worry about kittens. Still, I felt terrible that I let both Joe and Mama Thompson down.

It was about three months later when, one morning, as I was walking over to the Center, Mama Thompson came waltzing out of the woods, looking very pleased with herself. She appeared to be no worse for wear. Looking at each other warily, we came to an agreement, she and I. While she would acquiesce to be our cat, she would do so only as an outside one. She would agree to stay on the property, if, in exchange, we would provide her with food, water, and a heated shelter. We could do this. This agreement worked for many years. Darrell built a luxury condo with a front and back door, which sat on the front deck. It had two rooms, a dining room, and a bedroom; it was both heated and weatherproofed, and it even had a little covered porch. She loved it.

As time went on, Mama Thompson was the welcoming committee: greeting visitors, initially from a safe distance, and then, as she became more confident, even occasionally twining hesitantly around legs. She did what we called "the Marilyn Monroe," where she'd rub up against the deck railing, stretching one of her back legs out as if to say "check me out, will you?" She chased off the trespassing cats, but funnily enough, shared her bowl with the possum who moved in under the deck. During the winter storms, she would let us know if the electricity was out by standing in the front window box and complaining loudly that her heat wasn't working. The vet would visit her every so often to update her rabies vaccine; we had an elaborate system where the vet hid behind the door, and then just as the food was being put down, she'd step out for a quick jab. As she got more acclimated to us, we revisited the thought of convincing her to be an indoor cat. She reminded us during Hurricane Irene, however, that she was still a feral cat at heart. With horrible weather predicted, I was worried that she would have an awful time during the storm. Managing to trap her, I figured I could house her in the Center's Isolation Room and then let her back out when the storm was over. Once again, I was reminded of my flying monkeys.

As I opened the carrier door inside the Isolation Room, she let me know, with no uncertainty, that she would rather weather the storm outdoors. Scrambling up the Iso Room walls and across the ceiling in desperation to be let out, it was all I could do to get her back into a carrier. Not a problem, my mistake! Back to the outdoors she went, where she managed the awful weather without a hiccup.

Mama Thompson had been with us for a few years when she decided to invite a friend to stay. Over the years, several other cats had come to visit, but she always chased them away with a ferocity of ownership that was scary in itself. Graypuss, as he came to be known, was different

Graypuss

– maybe because he was young, certainly because he was male. A very cute and fairly well socialized eight-month-old grey cat with greenish eyes, he showed up one day, most likely a barn cat from one of the neighboring farms. Mama Thompson must have also thought he was cute, for he was allowed to share the front deck and surrounding property, as long as he remembered that she was the boss. He was not, however, invited into her cat condo.

As was true of all visiting cats on our property, we trapped him and had him neutered, then re-released him. Delighted to have a little attention, he hung around. He was an excellent hunter, whether this was to impress Mama Thompson or not, I don't know. He was always bringing bits and pieces of who knows what to share with her and to leave on our doorstep. With Graypuss, however, we felt bad – while Mama Thompson was perfectly happy to stay outdoors with her heated cabin on the deck, he was always trying to follow us indoors.

Additionally, he wasn't nearly as traffic savvy as she was, and could often be found hanging out near the volunteers' cars, even climbing in their open windows and sleeping on their backseats. While we would certainly have loved it if he inadvertently went home with someone, they might not have appreciated it, and as time went on, it became more and more apparent that we really needed to try to find a different situation for him. Because it was mid-summer, and all the shelters were teeming with cats and kittens, finding a home for this guy was not coming easily. I certainly wasn't going to be able to pass him off as a Siamese, being all grey with green eyes, that's for sure!

Then one day we got a phone call from a local lady who was looking to adopt. As I explained our program and talked about the type of cats we saw, she hemmed and hawed a bit. What she was really looking for was a cat that would not only be her buddy but could do double-duty as a mouser. She lived in a very old farmhouse that was home to a lot of field mice in the winter time, and she had recently lost her cat that kept them at bay. Not that some Siamese aren't mousers, they are, but knowing whether or not they would be a mouser, given the opportunity, was not something we felt we could accurately predict. While we had the occasional lizard in the Center, we, fortunately, didn't have a problem with mice. And then the lightbulb went off – did it have to be a Siamese that she adopted? Because we had a fantastic, young, healthy, guaranteed mouser that we needed to find a home for, and would she be interested?

The next day, she came to visit Graypuss. It was a perfect match. She was delighted to have a known mouser who was not only healthy, but outgoing and friendly as could be, and we were delighted to have him find a home where he could be loved and adored inside.

Mama Thompson went on to live ten more happy years with us. Yes, it was always a bit sticky to explain to the adopters who visited that the cats we adopted out had to stay inside, when they were being greeted by this robust looking gal marching back and forth on our front deck. However, as we had learned the hard way, some cats are just not made to live indoors.

As Mama Thompson aged up, her kidneys started to show some compromise. She became a bit slower, a bit easier to pet. The last two years of her life, we were even able to get her into the vet for annual exams. It was during one such exam and dental work that we discovered she had oral cancer. She had become an institution at the Rescue Center, and her presence was sorely missed.

TRUTH OR CONSEQUENCES

What lessons have I learned by this time? Was it not to believe what someone tells you on the phone, or to ask more questions, or perhaps to ask for documentation when someone telephones saying they need help? Well, I'll admit it, early on I continued to make mistakes – or maybe it's just that I believed that most people are honest. And over the years in Rescue, I have discovered that while that may be true, there's the truth, and then there's the whole truth. They don't always match.

Early in Rescue most of our requests for help were coming in by the telephone. While many of the calls were from the various animal shelters, as the word spread, an equal number of requests came in from owners who had been referred to us, either by the shelter or perhaps by their veterinarian who had heard about us. One of our best marketing strategies was to contact every adopter's vet, sending them not only all of the cat's medical records but also a package of information about our organization. This brought us a lot of referrals – both people wanting to adopt, as well as those needing help with rehoming a cat.

At the start of Rescue, my inclination was to jump down the throat of anyone who even suggested they might give up a pet; over time I became immune to some of the many reasons given. Of course, many were legitimate – the new baby who was allergic, the economic crash and resulting need to move, the marking behaviors by a cat who just didn't mesh in a home with too many animals. On the other end of the spectrum, excuses such as "I'm no longer a cat person," "The cat is old and not accepting my new kitten," or "I'm getting a puppy instead," would still push me over the edge.

There were some reasons that were truly not to be believed. We once had an owner who gave up their fourteen-year-old cat because "she purred too much, and it was just too loud." Really, after fourteen years? Is that even possible? At times like this, my ability to remain polite and professional was really put to the test. Then there was the behavior of some of the owners who dropped off their cat at the Center. The owners you wanted to see were the ones that were absolutely bawling buckets of tears. I would always end up crying with them, and we'd hug as I promised to make sure their cat was well cared for. To me, this clearly indicated that the owner really loved the cat. There were other times, however, when the owner acted as if they were leaving their cat at summer camp – seriously. With a "have fun" type attitude and a wave as they got in their car, they'd speed off with a smile on their face. I could never quite understand that. We even had a few times where the owner wouldn't get out of the car – just handed us the cat through the window.

Over time, I've come to the conclusion it's a waste of our energy to judge these people. It's far more effective to put our energy into helping the cat by gathering whatever information we could, and then moving forward. What good does it do to get all worked up about a decision that someone else has made about their life? Not to mention that rehoming the cat, if the owner actually wants to do it, is something I've come to believe can be the best move in many instances. We've yet to have a cat that wasn't happier in a home where they were loved and adored than in the previous home where they were barely tolerated, or worse even, disliked.

It was a year or two after the Center had been completed when I got a call from a young couple asking if we could take in their two cats. Their jobs were sending them both overseas, and they had no family to step in. By now I knew to ask for some level of detail: I wanted to see that the cats were Siamese, but most importantly, that the cats were adoptable. I had my questions ready. Where did they get the cats? Did they have any paperwork? How old were they and what was their medical status? And were they nice cats – could they be held, did they like to be petted, were they people friendly, or people adverse? And they were definitely Siamese cats, right?

Yes to everything, I was told. The cats had been purchased at a pet store several years ago; they cost $350 each. They had all of the original paperwork. This was their first ever experience with Siamese, but they were lovely, they said – very nice cats: healthy, good habits, friendly and outgoing. They had really enjoyed them but were forced into a situation where they could no longer keep them.

Now, this was before smartphones abounded, and we relied heavily on the fax machine for incoming and outgoing paperwork. I was not about to make any more mistakes, so I had them fax me the paperwork from the pet store showing the history. Sure enough – two Siamese kittens - $350 paid for each. I was getting pretty good at this intake thing, right?

Despite being about five hours away, this couple was desperate, and they didn't care about the distance. They had tried countless other avenues to rehome their cats, and they were, like many people forced into rehoming pets, coming up to their deadline, leaving the country in just a few days. To their credit, they absolutely refused to take them to the local public shelter, knowing how crowded the public shelters were, and how stressed the cats would be. They loved these cats, and in trying to rehome them, had done all the things we typically suggest – checked with family and friends – posted notices at area vet offices – even placed an ad in the paper. They tried local rescue groups, but they were all full. They were both crying on the phone, just pleading for help. Well, tears get me every time, so we set up a time and day for them to bring the cats. I readied the cages, got folders ready, and did my usual prep work. Two nice Siamese, healthy, already bonded, they should place easily, I thought. We had several adopters looking for a bonded pair; this should be a piece of cake.

It was late afternoon by the time they arrived. Out they got, two people, two very large carriers in hand. "Bring them on upstairs to the check-in area," I said, "and we'll get them logged in."

We went upstairs, and, before even glancing in the carriers, I asked for the paperwork. Even though I had received it by fax already, I learned to check things in person whenever possible. The paperwork checked out, identical to what they had faxed. I was now ready to look at the cats. The owners opened the carrier doors, and out they came. Big bruiser cats: friendly, healthy, nice looking. Lovely, lovely, cats, except for one thing – I could not detect a drop of Siamese. These were two domestic shorthair cats – black and white. No brown coloring, no solid body color, no points. Blue eyes, yes, but despite what some people think, blue eyes does not necessarily mean the cat is Siamese. The couple was legitimately stunned. They assumed that because they had blue eyes, because the pet store gave them an assurance in writing that these cats were Siamese, and because they were charged such a fee (exorbitant at the time), that these were Siamese cats. They had been duped!

Yes, we took them in; I wasn't about to turn them away after their long drive with both of them, standing there, eyes filled with tears. Yes, we were even able to place them, for their age, health and wonderful personalities worked in their favor. (One thing that's nice about having a solid reputation when it comes to customer service, if you will, is that people will adopt from you for the service, not just for the cat.) It wasn't long before an adopter came along whose primary focus was on the program's reputation, not the breed of the cat. She was delighted with these two boys; they went on to live long and happy lives. And yes, from that point forward, if someone contacted us about rehoming a Siamese, we always asked for pictures. Now did that mean we never took in a non-Siamese again? Well, sometimes you have no say in the matter...

Animal Control had called from a neighboring rural county, one without much in the way of resources, not even a public shelter. They received a phone call from an owner who was forced to leave his home, and in doing so, he had left his three Siamese at a country retreat up in the mountains. Asking for the person's information, we made contact directly with the owner. Unable to understand (and probably just as well that we didn't know) the reason for abandoning the home, we were given directions to the house. True, once again we didn't get pictures in advance; however, he did give us a very detailed description of the three cats, and we felt very comfortable that they were Siamese. There was a male chocolate point named Kobe, a female chocolate point named Marilyn, and a blue point female named Mystique. He had left them on the front porch with bags of food and bowls of water to keep them going. All sorts of things were running through our head – was he running from the law? Were we going to find the place crawling with FBI agents?

A bit nervously, Darrell and I headed out to this very mountainous area of Virginia. The directions took us up a long winding road that ended at a gorgeous A-frame cabin on the side of a mountain. If it wasn't for the fact there was a lot of miscellaneous items scattered around (some garden furniture, a wheelbarrow of tools, etc.), this would be the kind of home that would have been featured in some fancy house and garden type magazine. There were no neighboring homes for miles around; this was a very isolated beautiful piece of property with a barn nearby.

The atmosphere was a little creepy, but even more so just plain sad. What in the world could have happened that forced this man to make such a hasty retreat from such a beautiful home?

We gathered our supplies. By now we knew to

have packed everything we needed: carriers to put the cats in, heavy gloves for handling crabby cats, blankets for tossing over scared cats, boots for tracking through who knows what, cat food in case we couldn't catch the cats and would have to leave food for them, traps, you name it. We were ready.

Climbing up the front steps, we reached a beautiful wrap around porch with a quite expensive looking telescope set up on one end. The front door to the home was unlocked, no response when we knocked. We could see that some furniture had been removed, but much of it appeared to still be in place. Things were somewhat dirty and dusty, and there was a broken window pane that allowed indoor access for the cats (and other creatures, I'm sure).

The side porch, while enclosed, was roughed-in and in fairly poor shape. Clearly, a variety of animals had been coming and going. There were torn screens, upended bags of cat food, and trash littered everywhere. A few minutes after we arrived, out came the most gorgeous looking, breeder-quality Siamese – the male, Kobe – obviously the welcoming committee. Delighted to have our attention, he eagerly accepted an invitation into the waiting cat carrier. Scouting around for the next one, we saw, peering from the rafters, a pair of eyes reflecting down at us. This was the chocolate point, Marilyn, another gorgeous cat. We managed to coax her down and get her into a carrier, then continued to look around. After about half an hour of calling, shaking bags of cat food and popping some cat food tins, we saw the blue female, Mystique, streak through the living room. Cautiously letting ourselves into the home, we made our way around a mishmash of leftover furniture, eventually herding her into a corner and from there, into a carrier. Gathering our belongings, we got ready to head out. Our work was done, or so we thought.

As we put the carriers in the car, we heard a noise coming from the direction of the barn. Oye. We had been told about the cats being abandoned. What was the possibility that there might have been other animals left behind? We just couldn't, in good faith, leave without checking through the barn to make sure there wasn't another animal stranded there. Gingerly, I approached each stall, holding my breath, absolutely terrified I was going to see a half dead critter laying somewhere. Peering in all corners, I thanked the powers that be that the barn appeared to be empty. I could just see us trying to load something like a starving goat into the car!

Back to the CRV I went where we had the back door open, and the cats loaded up. We both still had this feeling, however, sort of like being watched, so we stood there, hesitating. Just as we were about to give up the ghost, so to speak, from the side of the barn two identical looking calico cats came waltzing out. Friendly as could be, they rubbed up against our legs, meowing eagerly. They were quite portly, clearly well-fed on a diet of mice and who knows what else. Strutting around, it certainly appeared that they owned the place. What to do now? Before we could even make any kind of decision on these cats, they took matters into their own paws, and hopped up into the back of the car, settling down with an expectant look on their faces. Really? Obviously, they were determined not to be left behind.

Okay, so now we had five cats with us: three of them in carriers, and the two calicos looking like Cheshire cats who had just won the lottery. We had no idea what we were going to do with the calicos, but we would figure something out. Off we went; first stop our vet in Madison to get combo tests done (blood tests to make sure the cats were negative for Feline Leukemia and Feline Immunodeficiency Virus) and to have the cats looked over. All tests were negative, thank goodness, though both the calicos and one of the Siamese needed to stay overnight for dental work. Not a problem, we could swing back the next day and pick them up. Heading home with the remaining two, we got them settled in cages at the Center. With such a sad story behind them, and being drop-dead gorgeous Siamese, they were going to be easy to place.

The next day, I headed over to the vets to pick up the remaining three cats. As I walked into the office, a gentleman was lamenting to the receptionist about how he had just lost his barn cat, and he needed to find another one. Well, just maybe we could help with that. Would he be interested in two fully vetted calico cats? They would be ideal candidates. Sure enough, he was more than delighted, as were the calicos. A happy ending for everyone, except the owner of the cabin.

BONZAI!

Mama Thompson wasn't the only cat that gave our Workman's Comp a good workout. At this point in time, our evaluation process was well established. We had trained Intake Evaluators whose job it was to visit each cat being considered for the program and complete a formal evaluation. Evaluations included gathering any history on the cat, observing the cat from a distance to see how the cat behaved, checking the cat over for obvious medical conditions, noting anything in the environment that might provide clues about the cat, and most importantly, holding the cat to make sure that no aggression was observed. Physically holding the cat was, in hindsight, probably the best requirement we initiated – however, it's not foolproof, as was true in this case.

Bonzai, appropriately named as it would turn out, was a seal point male who was actually evaluated twice by one of our trained Intake

Evaluators. Initially, he had been found as a stray in Maryland, taken to the public shelter, and was being kept in a cage along with some feral cats. At that first evaluation, when removed from the cage by our volunteer, he was handled without much issue. Before we had the space to bring him in, however, he was adopted out by the shelter to a family, then returned shortly after that for not using the litterbox. He was reevaluated again for our program, and despite very dilated pupils, he made direct eye contact, allowed himself to be handled without any noted aggression, and appeared to be a good candidate for us. As soon as we had a foster space open up at the Rescue Center, we brought him into our program.

As always, ringworm remained one of our biggest concerns, particularly with a cat that had been a stray at one point. By now, word of mouth had really spread about our program, and we were lucky to have a steady flow of applications coming in. Cats were moving fairly quickly, sometimes out the door within two weeks from the time they came in. Initially, I tried to stick with a ten to fourteen-day quarantine period for each cat before bringing them out of the Isolation Room, wanting to make sure that they didn't contaminate the rest of the cats. Because the cats were in such high demand, however, in certain instances, I would speed up the integration. As long as I gave them an anti-fungal bath, ran a ringworm culture to check for ringworm spores, and didn't observe any lesions, I felt that the risk I took by integrating them into the

Group Living area early was worth it. Occasionally, doing this would bite us you know where, but for the most part, we were able to curb the spreading of any germs as well as manage the quick turnover of purrsonalities successfully. (We always told adopters to wait the full fourteen days before integrating if they wanted to have a successful cat-cat relationship.) Proceeding with a fast integration helped me in making very quick personality assessments about the cats. Because we focused so much on the match of cat personality to adopter's home, if we could integrate them within a few days, we could often move the cat to its adoptive home very quickly, making space for another rescue cat.

Every so often we would end up with mild sniffles going through the Center, but that was fairly easily dealt with. With ringworm, which is an opportunist, as long as we kept everything squeaky clean – bleaching cages daily, changing out litterboxes and bedding regularly, and ensuring the floors were regularly mopped - the likelihood of an outbreak decreased considerably, as there was little opportunity for any spores to "hang around." And we were exceptionally clean at the Center; we worked really hard at keeping everything pristine.

Out of all of these precautions, the cat bath, in my mind, remained the most important part of avoiding any kind of outbreak. Therefore, upon arrival, the first thing for Bonzai would be his fungal bath. Knowing he had been in a cage with other feral cats gave me pause, as it was highly likely he could be a ringworm carrier, so I would really need to spend some time during the bath scrubbing his fur down. By doing this, I would not only be checking for any ringworm lesions but also assessing his personality while in this stressful situation, to see how he behaved. This type of information, along with what we learned during the integration in Group Living, would dictate whether each cat was best suited for kids, needed a quiet home, handled stress well, and so on and so forth.

Our cats typically arrived on the weekends with one of our wonderful transport volunteers. On Saturdays, we had several Kennel Workers (our weekend volunteers) who came to help scrub cages, clean litterboxes and work with the cats. Our bathing station was upstairs. When intake cats were brought in the front door, they were brought directly upstairs where I waited, ready with shampoo and towels. Typically, I did this activity on my own without any volunteer help. Not only did I think it was a bit safer to have the cat by himself in a quieter environment, but I found it actually easier to handle the cat during a bath if there were no distractions.

When I put Bonzai into the sink, as happens with many cats, he froze, not moving much at all, quite stiff in a crouched position. Frozen stiff is actually better than wild struggling – much easier to handle the cat. I was soaping away, getting him well covered in the fungal shampoo which, to reach its maximum effectiveness, is supposed to remain on the coat for ten minutes - which is a very *long* time to keep a cat calm in a sink. Things were going along well, when, suddenly, out of the blue, Bonzai flipped out. He was done with this bathing business. The previously solidified cat became a writhing, seething, mass of angry fur. Water, lather, cat, and soon blood was flying everywhere – for, sure enough, my hands got in the way as I was trying to hold onto him. Sinking his teeth into my palm, he managed to bite almost completely through the base of my left index finger.

And *oh* did it hurt. I have been bitten many different times in my career, but this one felt so much more painful than the others, way outclassing the discomfort of the Mama Thompson experience. I was spouting obscenities while Bonzai was flying around the room, a very wet and traumatized cat. Luckily for both of us, there were no other cats around, all the doors were closed, and there was nowhere for him to go. I called to the volunteers downstairs for help, asking them to get Darrell who was next door in the house. The first priority was to catch Bonzai. Armed with blankets, together we managed to corner him by tossing a blanket over him and doing what I called a pillow wrap, where you encase the cat in the blanket. We were then able to plunk him in a cage. Meantime I rinsed the bite on my hand, doused it with peroxide, and started some antibiotics (which I had learned to keep on hand for occasions such as this).

Several weeks went by. Despite the passage of time and a calm and quiet environment, Bonzai remained hunkered down in the corner, hissing and swatting whenever approached. After a few more weeks, we moved him down to the Group Living environment, a large room filled with cat furniture where ten to twenty cats live communally at any one time. Each cat has their own cage with a litterbox in which they are closed up at night. During the day they can leave (or not) their cages as they so wish and interact (or not) with the other cats in the room. For cats who are not very well socialized, this type of environment often works well. They can watch (and hopefully model) the other cats as they interact with humans; they can progress at their own pace with respect to their socialization, and they have access to their own private space if they so choose.

Bonzai stayed with us for several months. Unfortunately, rather than become more relaxed, he became more and more stressed in the Group Living environment. He started picking on both the males and females, to the point that we had to let him out by himself at night when the other cats were caged. And then he started spraying. Spraying is actually something that both males and females can do even after they have been spayed or neutered. It is usually due to either stress or the need to claim their territory. Once one cat starts spraying, it often sets off a chain reaction, and before you know it, multiple cats are spraying. Then, of course, the adoptions come to a standstill, as no one wants to take on a cat with a history of spraying.

After careful consideration and a lot of discussions, we decided that Bonzai would be happier in a sanctuary environment where he could spray to his heart's content. We managed to pillow wrap him again and transferred him to the local animal sanctuary that we had a long-term relationship with.

In the meantime, while my hand had healed up, I continued to have very little sensation in my index finger. It was numb and tingly from the middle of the finger to the end; I was constantly dropping things when I tried to use my left hand. So back I went to the local physician.

Now living in a rural part of Virginia certainly has some benefits, but let me warn you, it doesn't always attract the most experienced in the medical field. My physician was a very nice lady, and I'd been seeing her routinely for some time, but when she told me, after examining my hand, that I'd likely always have some numbness and loss of feeling in that finger and there wasn't much that could be done, I wasn't buying it. If that were true, I'd never be able to safely scruff another cat to give it a bath. Informing her that the status quo was unacceptable, I got a referral to the hand surgeon who treated hand injuries for the UVA football team. He discovered the nerve in my palm had been severed and immediately scheduled me for reconstructive surgery. Several months later, my hand was pretty much back to normal, and Bonzai had settled happily into life at the sanctuary.

This wasn't, by any means, the only time that the local physician's group let us down. Not long after this experience, Darrell came down with what we thought was the flu. Now in my experience, men aren't the most robust when it comes to being sick, and it wasn't too many days into his misery that I was finding it really hard to remain sympathetic. Whatever he had come down with just dragged on and on and on, as did the moaning and groaning and genuine mutual discomfort. When he finally went to the doctor (novel idea, right?), even they could not put their finger on what this was. It wasn't until after a number of repeated visits and several blood tests later that it turned out Darrell had the dubious honor of being the first ever in our rural county to contract Cat Scratch Fever. A bacterial infection that comes from a bite or a scratch from an infected cat, this is akin to a really bad flu, and can certainly make one feel really awful. I had to eat a lot of crow on that one!

Being bitten by a cat is never fun – but being bitten by a personal cat, or a cat with a known history is an entirely different ball of fur than being bitten by a cat from an unknown background. Remember that, in Rescue, we're talking about many cats that were strays, turned into shelters, and then transferred to us. These cats were outside and could have been exposed to who knows what. While ringworm is one thing, rabies, on the other hand, is more serious. Cats that come off the streets obviously have an unknown vaccination history, and while most shelters do vaccinate the cats for rabies before releasing them to an owner or a rescue group, the vaccine is not immediately effective. Our next experience with a biting cat made it clearly apparent that we needed to be quite a bit more insistent about gathering information from the releasing agent. Just how dangerous things could get when you haven't been given all of the information became quite obvious.

We were called to help with a cat that was at a shelter in Connecticut. When we asked for the history on the cat, very little information was provided. All we were told was that he was a five-year-old seal point named Sammi that had been turned into the shelter by someone. We sent out an Evaluator to visit with the cat; he got high marks on the evaluation as he wound around her legs and purred up a storm. He seemed to be a perfect candidate for the newest Foster joining our team, and so in he came to the program.

Our foster mom was able to bathe him without any problems. She got started on his medical write up, made some notes, and was eagerly working on getting pictures and his web blurb done so she could add him to the website and start looking for an adopter. Along with her ten-year-old daughter, the two of them spent that first evening in the bedroom with Sammi, loving on him, playing with him, and in general gathering information she could share with the adopters as she began the matchmaking process to find him just the right family. It was in the midst of their evening visit that Sammi, without any warning, flipped a switch – turning, quite unexpectedly, from a lap-sitting, outgoing cat, to an aggressive biter. No, not just a nip, but a serious bite for both of them that sent them to the emergency room, where they received medical attention and started on antibiotics. Unfortunately, that was not the end of it.

After returning home from the hospital, the foster mom peeked in to check on Sammi, wanting to make sure his food, water, and litterbox were set up for the night. Following our foster protocols, she had notified me of the incident, and I had suggested she leave Sammi in the closed bedroom, allowing him time to chill and recover from the experience as well. (More often than not, cats are equally traumatized after a bite incident, and need a cooling down period.) When she checked Sammi, however, he was not cooling down at all, but rather was acting extremely agitated, circling with his head tilted to one side. His eyes were dilated, and he kept up a stream of long guttural howls. The Foster fed him quickly and let him be as instructed, hoping he'd chill out overnight. The next day, however, he was still demonstrating the same behaviors, and when she entered the room, he charged again. Despite a cookie sheet and oven mitts, Sammi was able to grab her arm once again.

Our biggest concern, at this point, with the odd behavior that Sammi was demonstrating, was that we might be dealing with rabies. While Sammi had come from the shelter with a recently administered rabies vaccine, it had only been given a few days previously. We had been given little background information about Sammi, and we were worried about the worst-case scenario.

Unfortunately, there is only one way to test for rabies in animals, and it involves euthanizing them. Rabies is a disease that is not only fatal to the animal but can be very serious to the person who gets bitten without immediate vaccine protection. After much discussion with the vet, and because Sammi continued to show both strange and aggressive behaviors, we decided the safest thing to do was to go ahead and test him for rabies. While the incidence of rabies in cats is very low, we didn't feel we could take any chances. The test would take three days; if positive, we would get the Foster to the doctor immediately to start the series of vaccines.

Was there any good news about this experience? A little: Sammi was negative for rabies, meaning the Foster and her daughter were in the clear; they recovered, successfully fostering many other cats after that; and we now knew to make much more of a fuss if we were told there was no turn-in paperwork. The bad news, of course, was that we lost Sammi in the process. When I called the director at the shelter that Sammi had come from and relayed the series of events we had just experienced, I was hit with the final blow – just *a little late* in the game. As it turned out, Sammi had been returned to the shelter multiple times for biting aggressively; that turn-in paperwork with those details had somehow gotten waylaid and was never given to us, even though we asked.

If we had only had this information early on, things might have turned out very differently for everyone concerned. It was, of course, terribly upsetting to lose Sammi; we felt, however, that if we were going to make a tough decision, we had to err on the side of safety.

BLOOD AT THE OFFICE

Throughout our Rescue experience, there were many other times one of us got chomped on. It was rarely a laughing matter, although there was one experience with a cat named Snowbear that, in hindsight, gave us a good chuckle!

Rescue had been running out of the Center for about a year. The Center, being on our personal property in the two-car garage looking building, was about 100 feet out of the front door. As anyone who works out of their home knows, there are all sorts of perks that come with this type of set up – it really was ideal. Once we had the Center built, I could be "working from home" but still technically leave the house – I had all of a one-minute commute. Even during times of awful weather, if I had to, I could bundle up in my pajamas and make it next door to feed the cats, scoop the litterboxes, and wash down the cages with only a minimal amount of outdoor exposure.

Of course, the pajama parties stopped after Darrell had been here a year or two, for being the super tech wizard he is, he had installed webcams to allow adopters to see the cats. The cameras made me much more conscious about what I was wearing. The importance of my outfits was clearly apparent one day when I was over at the Center, working away, and I got a phone call from one of our regular weekend volunteers. She was in Florida visiting her 90-year-old father; for fun, she had pulled up the Center Webcam and was showing him where she volunteered on the weekends. It wasn't the Center set up, or even cats that interested him - he had a much more pressing concern. What in the world, he wanted to know, was I wearing on my feet? (It was mid-winter in Virginia, and I was wearing some very funky socks and a pair of flip flops.)

Over the years, we had some very funny phone calls in response to the cameras. There was the time one of our weekend volunteers lifted her shirt to show a good friend her mastectomy scar, not realizing she was standing in front of a camera. Another time someone called to ask if Darrell felt alright because he was looking very tired. And then there was the woman who was in an absolute panic because there was a black cat stuck on the roof of the Center, and we had to get a ladder out immediately. (It was the weathervane.) And those were the things we knew people had seen. We have to wonder about some of the other embarrassing things we hoped (like hell) no one noticed. More on that in a later chapter!

By this time, I had my daily routine set up. While I was enjoying no longer having that one-hour drive to and from work, I was at this point divorced and working at Rescue fulltime, and despite all the benefits, I was feeling a bit discouraged. My days, every day, seven days a week, were much the same – I was spending a great deal of my time scooping poop, cleaning up puke and intervening in cat squabbles. I'd wander back and forth between the house and the Center, taking care of the physical work of Rescue next door, coming back to the house to work on the computer and make phone calls. It was certainly convenient, but after a while, I really felt isolated. Had all my education and work experience come to this? Four years of college, two years of graduate school, and I was scooping litterboxes? (My mother was wondering about this as well.) Adoptions were solid, but almost all adopters visited on Saturdays, leaving the other days empty. We hadn't yet developed our extensive network of volunteers, so there was no Kennel Crew coming to help with the Center chores on the weekends. Almost all of the adult social interactions I had were at night, discussing the various website changes with Darrell over the phone or on email. We live in a very rural community, and while we have neighbors, I'm not close friends with any of them. My new routine was all day, every day, the same thing again and again. Sweatpants and t-shirts, grunge Mom at her best, I was starting to feel a bit sorry for myself.

So what to do? I needed to come up with some way to boost myself up – to make myself feel better about what was, in actuality, a pretty idyllic set-up. If I could just paint the situation with a different brush, look at it differently, maybe I'd feel a little better. And then it occurred to me that there was no reason at all why I couldn't psych myself out – I had plenty of office experience in my past to pull from. All I had to do was change my outlook. Now that the Center had been built, I would develop an "office" routine, and every day, prior to leaving the house to walk the short distance to the Center, I would shower, dress up just a bit, add a touch of make-up, and act as if I was heading off to work. While I'd still spend the day in the company of cats, and still be scooping pans, I could set up my computer over there and pretend it was my office. This, I figured, would help myself feel a little better about life as it was. I even went out and bought myself a new outfit to wear – something still suited to working with cats, but much nicer than the grungy clothes I typically wore.

Monday came around: day one of my new routine. I got Nicole up and off to school, came back, had my second cup of coffee and got ready for work. I donned my new outfit – a button-up long-sleeved white dress shirt and a nice pair of slacks – not too fancy, but a big improvement over the scrubs and sweats I had been accustomed to wearing. Determined to spend as much of the day next door as I could, rather than traipse back and forth between house and Center, I gathered up all I needed for my new office situation. I had set up a desk and computer in the little dormer section of the upstairs, where the window provided a lovely view of the Blue Ridge Mountains. I already had a fridge over there for the cat medications, so I even packed a sandwich for lunch. I was ready for my first full official day at the office, and was convinced that this would be the ticket to feeling a bit more positive about my job in Rescue.

The upstairs where I set up my work station was an area I used for the shyer cats. The majority of the cats were kept downstairs in Group Living. Initially, when we opened the Center, I had the cats downstairs out of their cages all the time. I would put down several bowls of dry food for them to munch on and then serve wet food, individually, twice a day. I quickly realized that the fat cats got fatter, the timid cats got thinner, and the cats with delicate stomachs vomited everywhere. So I changed from "herd feeding" over to individual food bowls, which worked very well for the remaining years of Rescue. I also assigned every cat their own cage, which, I found increased their level of security.

After a cat's initial isolation time (bath and ringworm culture included), if the cat was outgoing, I would move the cat downstairs to Group Living. Here, they would be assigned a cage based on their needs. Fat cats and timid cats would get a floor-level cage, as both types were unlikely to be comfortable jumping up and down; the very spry, young, athletic cats got a top-level cage, as they were nimble enough to climb up high, and the rest were assigned to a middle- level cage. Each cat kept their cage from start to finish (i.e., entry into Group Living until adoption). At night, every cat would be put in their assigned cage with their food and water, bedding and litterbox. This gave each cat a nice balance between private time and public time. It also allowed us not only to supervise the food, but also to feed different types of food based on the needs of the cat. This way we could observe how much each cat was eating and would also be able to see what was being produced in the litterbox.

During the day, with their cage doors open, the cats could come and go as they pleased. Having an area to call their own really helped with their level of comfort, some cats choosing to remain in their cage throughout the day, others anxious to leave first thing in the morning. Having both private and public time seemed to lessen any territoriality issues that would crop up, as it became clear which cat owned what space, if you will. Of course, that didn't stop the very obnoxious cats from immediately exiting their cage first thing in the morning and visiting everyone else's litterbox, in an attempt to make a statement. With most of the cats being adopted within a few weeks, there was rarely enough time for any cat to establish a place on the hierarchy chain, and everyone got along.

Trouble would arise, however, with any cat that overstayed his welcome. After the first few weeks of what I termed a "honeymoon" type period (during which visitors would marvel at how the cats would all appear to coexist), conflicts would sometimes become apparent. It always seemed to be between the six- and ten-week mark when those cats who hadn't been adopted yet started to lay claim to the public domain territory. Even then, peace could still be maintained, provided there were no fraidy cats in the bunch. But as I had quickly come to learn, fear triggers aggression, and the minute the long-termer started to flex his authority, the fraidy cat(s) would suffer. Just like in the human world of bullying, the bully cat feeds off of the response of their victim – and when a cat runs in fear, it would provoke the bully cat to take chase. Fortunately, for the most part, with the rapid turnover we didn't run into this type of behavior all that often.

Working away at my computer upstairs, I had been "at my office" for about an hour when I heard some cat keening coming from Group Living. Jumping up from the desk, I rushed downstairs to see what was going on.

Entering Group Living, I saw two cats standing in a face-off: Snowbear and Warlock. Snowbear was a male blue point who had come into our program during the first few months the Center was open; he was one of the sixty-eight cats we took from the hoarding disaster in Fairfax County. He had been with us for a couple of months and was managing alright, although I had started to notice an increase in his pacing behavior: we were at the start of some hierarchy issues. Each day, he would seem a bit more anxious about the Group Living situation; he was slowly starting to show more and more of a tendency to bully the other cats. As I went running down the stairs and entered the room, I could see him pacing back and forth in his (open) cage on the middle level, looking quite agitated. Warlock, a young male seal, sat on the floor, staring up at him. Both cats were posturing – their necks were arched and bent to the side, their ears were back, the fur along the spine and tail was standing up on end. Tails were a-twitching. The low growling was escalating into some higher pitched caterwauling.

Snowbear

Grabbing the Super Soaker squirt gun (which I always kept filled and ready to use), I shot a stream of water first at one at, then at the other. Unfortunately, this had little effect, and the cat calls, or banshee chicken noises as I liked to call them, continued to escalate. Snowbear pounced from above, claws and teeth bared; Warlock responded in kind. What followed was my first very scary experience of being in the middle of a group of agitated cats.

When there is a cat fight within a group of cats, some of the cats will tuck their tails between their legs and run away, finding something to hide under until the threat has passed. Others, however, will run towards the fight, agitated by the sounds and smells, and join in the fracas. Before I knew it, there were not just two, but four bundles of fur, rolling head over heel with a great deal of very ferocious sounding vocalizations. Squirting like crazy, screaming at the top of my lungs, and grabbing cat bedding to throw at the melee, I managed to break the cats apart – for a minute. Before I could catch my breath, however, Snowbear had shifted his focus to me and was now heading towards me at full force. Launching himself at my leg, he grabbed on as if he was straddling a tree trunk - with all four paws, and his teeth, sinking deeply into my thigh. As I frantically shook my leg, trying to dislodge him, there was an enormous ripping sound. Snowbear went flying, taking most of the leg of my new pair of slacks with him. There was blood spatter everywhere, mostly mine, and it wasn't long before my new white blouse was red polka-dotted.

I finally managed to get everyone calmed down, and back in their cages. Throwing blankets over cats who are upset works quite well if you can get them fully covered with one, as they tend to freeze, not knowing which direction to head. I checked everyone over, the cats seemed to be fine – I had definitely born the brunt of this skirmish. It was nothing that band-aids and a little hydrogen peroxide wouldn't fix, although that new outfit was definitely headed for the garbage bin. So much for my "office experience." It was overwhelmingly clear to me that this was nothing like an office, and while I could pretend all I wanted to, the reality was that bleachable old clothes were a much better choice. That was the last time I ever wore nice clothes to work over at the Center!

Even after weeks of working with him, Snowbear couldn't be rehabilitated. He remained highly unpredictable and volatile, and as such was a liability to place. Sometimes, unfortunately, Rescue just can't fix the cat. One would like to think that even the cats whose psyches have been seriously damaged by whatever atrocity they previously faced, will eventually come around. Unfortunately, the truth is that sometimes the cat is too broken, and the rescue environment only makes them worse. It can be a catch-22, because while such a damaged cat might come around given a long enough time in the right situation, that environment is rarely a shelter type environment, but a home. At the same time, placing a rescue cat who is known to be aggressive with an adopter is a real liability.

Before we knew to scrutinize what cats we accepted into the program, we often ended up with some cats that just weren't placeable. Even after we had trained Evaluators, despite a thorough evaluation, we'd still, at times, end up with cats that were not adoptable. There was Wheeler, who had been raised in a house that was full of Pitbulls being used for dogfighting. Wheeler had learned, early on, that whenever there was any kind of chaos – be it a cat squabble, a dog barking, or, gosh forbid, a child crying – that the best defense was a good offense, and he would launch himself at whatever was going on, trying to get the upper hand before it got him. Because of this behavior, he was not a cat we felt safe placing. There was Remington, a cat who had lived his entire life outdoors competing for territory, and when put in an indoor-only environment, sprayed everything in sight. He went to three different homes (we tried both with other cats and without other cats), and he still sprayed. Thank goodness we have a well-run animal sanctuary nearby. All three of these cats (Snowbear, Wheeler, and Remington) were transferred there and went on to live out their lives in an environment that was much better suited to their needs. As for me, from that point forward, I stayed in sweatpants or scrubs.

THE YIN AND YANG

People are always asking "Why did you choose to rescue Siamese?" There's no single answer to that other than if your mother loved something, and then you grew up with that something, it seems to become a part of you. My family always loved Siamese: the intelligence, the dog-like quality of following you everywhere, the sensitive nature. Of course, that sensitivity can be both a blessing and a curse, often leading to the intense range of emotions that can be seen within the Siamese breed. Some of the most difficult cats we encountered in Rescue were either very, very angry, or very, very sad, and because of this, it was often very hard to get through to them.

One Friday evening we got a call pleading for help. I had just arrived home from my teaching job and was getting ready to start "the rounds." Having gotten my name from the shelter one county over, Mrs. B. had found a large male Siamese cat rambling around her back yard. Assuming he belonged to a neighbor, she watched his health slowly decline over several days while waiting for his owner to take action. By Thursday morning, the cat could barely walk. His chest rose and fell as he struggled to clear his airway from whatever goops and ganders had settled therein. No longer able to stand the discomfort this poor guy was obviously experiencing, Mrs. B. found an old crate in her garage and made him a small shelter. Despite the evening hour, she begged me to come take a look, so I did.

When I arrived, I found all eleven saggy pounds of Tiki hunched into a corner of the crate, looking really miserable. His lips hung in a rumpled fashion on his face, and his eyes streamed water. A gurgling sound could be heard with every breath, and *oh*, those eyes! So very sad and soulful. Bundling him into a large carrier, I called the vet. By now, she was familiar with these last minute "fit-ins," and hearing his story, she agreed to stay late until I got to the office. Heading straight there, I cringed with each raking breath he took, his snortling easily heard over the car's engine.

Ushering us in right away, the vet hummed and hawed, poked and prodded, examined and injected. He had a fractured pelvis, horrendous dental disease, and had been neglected for so long, he was bone thin under all those folds of fur. Armed with a small pharmacy, I headed home with the understanding I had to convince Tiki to eat, or there would be no hope. His fractured pelvis would heal itself, the extensive dental could be done at a later date. The immediate concern was getting him some nourishment and building up his strength. Without their sense of smell, many cats go into a slump and literally starve themselves to death, and this was a highly probable outcome if he didn't start eating.

On top of that, his teeth were in such poor condition that his mouth must have hurt like crazy, and who wants to eat when your mouth hurts. Unfortunately, there was no way he was strong enough to withstand surgery to remove all the infected teeth that were in there, so the best we could hope was that the antibiotics and pain meds would be enough to convince him to try. A large-boned cat, his skin was draped around him, and his expression reminded me of a defeated soldier. The vet felt that his injuries were most likely from a throw or a fall from a moving car; the human rejection and physical trauma were painfully obvious not only in his physical condition but in his emotional state as well.

Now, this was before the Center had been built, so the cats were isolated in one of the various rooms in the house. Tiki got the upstairs middle bathroom. Covering the floor with soft towels, I felt confident in my ability to offer an appetizing cuisine. Having rescued cats now for several months, I had all the mainstays in the cupboard: various gourmet cat foods, wet and dry, baby foods, tuna, canned shrimp and sardines, chicken breast, scrambled eggs. By now I knew that with some of these cats you had to keep a continual Lazy Susan of offerings provided, until you found just the right one that would tempt their palate.

Over the next twenty-four hours, I exhausted all those possibilities and then some. Tiki lay in a crumpled heap, showing not the slightest interest in anything put in front of him. His breathing was so loud and labored it could be heard through the door, putting Kevin's snoring to shame. Humidifiers, Eucalyptus oil, Vicks – nothing seemed to make the slightest bit of difference.

By Sunday, I realized I was going to lose him if I didn't do something drastic. But what to do? My attempts at syringe feeding were failing miserably. I'd syringe the baby food into his mouth, and he'd make no efforts to swallow. The food would dribble out all over his fur, and unlike Mariah, he couldn't care less about cleaning himself up. He was so depressed that he was completely uninterested in anything around him. Even a fishy calorie supplement on my finger, inserted into his mouth, dribbled out with no interest. Attempts to play had been futile, petting and brushing him evoked little response. The situation did not look hopeful at all.

Figuring it was close to impossible to make the situation much worse, I decided to ignore all the physical ailments he was dealing with and aim specifically at his psyche. Armed with towels, heaters, a blow dryer, shampoo, Q-tips and nail clippers, I drew a long, warm bath. Gathering Tiki up, I lowered him gently in. Despite knowing that the vet would likely have a stern reprimand for me, and that there could very possibly be a negative effect on Tiki's health, particularly with that fractured pelvis, I began soaping. Tiki lay like a rag doll, not having the strength to give even the slightest bit of protest. I gently scrubbed and rinsed, soaped and soaked. The sweat trickled down my neck as the heater warmed the air to a steamy ninety-five degrees. Tiki molded to my hands in whatever form I needed, barely flicking a whisker as the bubbles enveloped his body. As I continued to scrub, a dim light began to glow in Tiki's eyes. Stretching his neck, his tongue raked across my hand. A muffled sound came from his throat - a very weak attempt to purr. Never had I seen a cat luxuriating in warm, soapy water before. His eyes half closed, his body relaxed; a look of sheer contentment crossed his face.

Fifteen minutes later, after soaping him ears to paws and rinsing him well, I lifted him onto the softest towel I could find. Rubbing him briskly, the reality of the possible impact of what I had done to a cat with severe congestion and a fractured pelvis sank in. For all I knew, I could be sending him into a rapid decline. Of course, it was Sunday and miles to an emergency vet, so if I had further damaged his pelvis, I'd be in a boatload of trouble. Yet right before my eyes, Tiki was quickly becoming a changed cat. Slowly he purred and stretched, arched and yawned, and when he couldn't stand it any longer, took a paw in helping with the clean-up. Licking both himself and then me, he began to purr full throttle.

Next came the blow dryer. Tiki loved this and stood stock still while I blew and brushed and fluffed him clean. We finished with a nail trim and ear cleaning, and the once sad-looking Meezer was now a silky, handsome bundle of contentedness. I could almost see the positive energy flow through his limbs as to my delight, he lumbered over to the food bowl and began eating like there was no end in sight.

Twelve weeks later, I was packing Tiki's things for his trip up north. He had made a remarkable recovery. His hip had healed as best as it was going to – he walked with a bit of a swagger and still had some trouble with the stairs, but seemed to be fairly comfortable. He was sleeping in my daughter's arms every night, crawling into our laps while we watched television, smiling at us with that silly toothless grin he had. He recovered without a hitch from the sixteen extractions that he needed. He showed an incredible appreciation of everything one gave him, and there wasn't a food type he didn't like. Tiki had filled out most of his folds and blossomed into a handsome, distinguished gentleman. While the vet's face had initially reflected some disapproval when I described the bath episode, she was astonished at the change and improvement she saw.

Tiki went to live with Cheryl and Steve in upstate

New York, happily settling in with his new family and his best friend, Pippin. Cheryl called him a "marshmallow of a cat" and I couldn't agree more – hugging him was nothing less than a soft, squishy and feel-good experience. Sometimes you've got to go with your gut, and in his case, starting on the inside and working my way out, focusing on his emotional state, was his ticket to recovery.

Tiki was for sure one of those potential soulmate cats, but surprise, I didn't keep him. One thing that carried over from my training as a special education teacher – I found that the cats I really identified with were always the ones with major issues. Perhaps it was because they were with us for a long time before getting adopted and we grew so attached to them, or maybe it was because I had invested so much emotion and time into trying to pull them through, that we had bonded so tightly. I finally understood the concept of Rescue – what comes in, needs to go back out.

On the opposite end of the spectrum was another absolutely wonderful cat that I also didn't end up keeping – Sebastian. He was, without a doubt, one of the angriest cats in all the years of Rescue. Despite his attitude, I sure adored this cat.

Sebastian came to us in a very circuitous way. We had gotten a call from an older lady in Northern Virginia whose son had passed away from HIV, and she had taken in his cat. The cat, a middle-aged curmudgeon of a seal point male, wanted nothing to do with her. He was angry, spiteful, and quite the handful. While fortunately he was eating and litterboxing without an issue, every time she approached him, he would swat and lash out. Madeline asked if I could come and visit – hoping we could take this cat. The story in itself was so sad – I felt terrible for Madeline, having lost her son, and of course felt awful for the cat, having lost his person. So up I drove to Northern Virginia to do a home visit, where I came face-to-face with a twelve-pound ball of fairly perturbed Siamese sass. Madeline, a real cat lover, already had one cat, a female, and trying to manage the two cats in a small one-bedroom apartment, when one of them was being just plain nasty to her, was leaving her in tears. Clearly, she was quite frightened of Sebastian, and he was capitalizing on this. Of course, she also felt awful as Sebastian had been her son's cat, and she felt a real obligation to her son to make sure he was well cared for. Was there any way at all we would consider a trade, she queried? She'd like to have another cat to keep her cat company, but she just didn't think that she could manage with Sebastian.

I had to agree. Neither owner nor cat was happy in this situation. So once again, without considering how adoptable he might be (or not), I cornered Sebastian and got him into a large carrier and headed back to the Rescue. It didn't take long until we found a suitable male for her to adopt instead – a young, easygoing fluffy seal point – and we made the trade official. Madeline was so very appreciative, and what stuck with me was that she named this one Sebastian as well!

Meantime, back to Sebastian #1. The first thing to do was to get him to the vet, no easy task. If I thought he had been angry in Madeline's home, he was really angry at being brought to the Center, not to mention having to be caged with so many other cats wandering around. He was so fractious that by the time we managed to get him to the vet, even the vet questioned as to whether we really thought this guy was an adoptable pet. At the vet visit, however, it turned out that poor Sebastian had a very infected mouth. Dental care is the one area that we have repeatedly seen lacking in many of the middle to older aged cats we get, and in my opinion, is one of the primary reasons every cat should visit a vet annually, at a minimum. There aren't too many pet owners who are adept at opening their cat's mouth and examining not just those front teeth, but those back molars in depth, and I would venture to say that the majority of cats (no different from humans) need dental care at some point in their lives. It was not uncommon for a cat to be turned into us and to need ten to twenty extractions. Imagine living with that many cavities and abscesses in your mouth! That level of discomfort boggles my mind, and it certainly makes sense that it could cause some behavior issues. Anyway, there was no doubt Sebastian was a prime candidate for dental work, and I could only hope that this would improve his personality significantly.

While the twelve necessary extractions certainly

helped him feel better, he remained quite the grump. He just was none too pleased with his circumstances: starting with the loss of his owner, then the move to the small apartment with another cat, followed by the move to the Center, then to the vet for all that dental work, then back to the Center, and still without a home.

It was early in our application screening process, and I was doing much of the screening and interviewing of prospective adopters. I won't hesitate to tell you that I wasn't very good at it. I hated talking on the phone and I didn't yet know to ask the probing questions. I tended to take everyone at their word (remember I'm Pollyanna), and I was somewhat naïve, always thinking people would act in the same way I would have. When I got a serious inquiry into Sebastian from a woman in Chicago, after lots of emails and phone calls, I was convinced this was the right situation for him. Turning to one of our volunteers who had airline privileges, we arranged for Sebastian to travel, in cabin, from Dulles to O'Hare, and despite the funny look the vet gave me when we got his health certificate (she still wasn't buying that this cat was adoptable), I felt good that his placement was a solid one.

Did I mention I stink at interviewing? This was the reason it became clear early on in the organization that we needed to find some top-quality volunteers, experienced in this area, who could be tasked with the very important job of screening our applicants. Just like the other volunteer jobs in our organization, the interviewing process went through a lot of changes. By the time we were several years into Rescue, we had a really solid training program and an incredible Interviewer Team. Too bad this was not in place early on, because it wasn't forty-eight hours after Sebastian landed in Chicago that the adopter called me up and told me to come to get him, that he was just way too grumbly and growly for them. Easy to ask for but a bit more difficult to implement. Unfortunately, we had no one to fly with him this time around as we were pressed for time, so he had to fly in pet cargo back to Dulles. First problem was that it was a connecting flight. Second problem was that it was back when the airlines didn't provide any means of tracking the animal during the flight. Third problem was that the second flight was delayed. Poor Sebastian was, needless to say, supremely agitated. He ended up sitting on the tarmac for a bit with no personal attention, and we had no way to find out how he was doing. Finally, he was loaded onto that second flight and arrived back at Dulles. A lot of mistakes on my part (we would never use pet cargo again), and the entire experience certainly didn't help Sebastian's attitude. I was so very glad to have him back safe and sound.

Fortunately, this story does have a very happy ending. Sebastian came back to the Center, settling back into the routine. Sometimes, I have discovered, cats actually do better the second time around in an environment, perhaps something to do with the familiarity. He was with us for quite a few months after that first placement, and he finally got the hang of both the Center and of Adoption 101, as we like to call it. As a grumbly yet likable middle-aged gent, he eventually caught the eye of two of our Kennel Workers, a husband and wife who volunteered on the weekends. They loved him from the start, managed his grumbling with compassion and care, moved with him several times, and shared wonderful pictures of him through the years as he finally let down his guard and became a well-adored family member.

WHY DO MY SOULMATES ALWAYS NEED DIAPERS?

Over time, I was finally getting the hang of adopting out the cats even if I had become really attached to them. Actually, it's interesting, while one would think someone like me would fall deeply in love with each and every cat, that's actually not true. Believe it or not, some cats actually drive me a bit crazy; there are others that fall into the "okay" category. Some cats are amazing, but for me only a few actually make it to soulmate status. This took me quite a while to realize. I thought that if I found a nice cat, and loved it enough, that cat would become my soulmate. Remember how I got Kipper, thinking he would be my soulmate, and then Suki, thinking she'd fill the spot, and then Duke auditioned for the role? All wonderful cats, but none of them making it to that top tier.

By the way, after observing my own behavior over the years, I realize that had I been on the other side of the adoption process, I'd be a real headache to deal with as an adopter. There is no doubt my continual search for a soulmate would have driven our wonderful Fosters around the bend. Look at all of the cats I had to go through before finding a soulmate.

I overdid it a bit in the canine department as well. One of the adopters I met during the first few years of Rescue was a big Italian Greyhound fan. She went on and on about these dogs (affectionately known as Iggys), telling me how much they were like Siamese cats in their personality. I really should get one, she kept saying. Getting on the internet, I took a look at the Italian Greyhound Rescue groups. Why not fill out an application online, I thought, and *no*, I didn't tell Kevin. The application clearly stated that there was a several month waitlist to get a dog, so I figured I had plenty of time to come up with an excuse. Yikes! This was not at all true, for when the Director of the Iggy Rescue group saw that I too was involved in Rescue, she bumped my name to the top of the list. Not two weeks later, I was approved, and my dog was waiting for me in Eastern TN. (Um, Kevin, guess what?) Figuring I should get a perk here and there as the Director of Siamese Rescue, I asked the Meezer Express Team if they would be willing to transport my rescued Iggy up to the Central Virginia area, and they were.

On the designated day and time, my mother and I were eagerly waiting in the Cracker Barrel parking lot for the transport to arrive. Up drove the Transporter, and peeking out of the back seat sat little Dixie. And my comment to my mother? "Oh my goodness, that's the ugliest dog I have ever seen." I knew very little about this breed. I had never met one. I had not done any research. I was just going on what someone else told me. Yes, I was a completely uninformed adopter. That having been said, years later, I absolutely adore this breed, still have one today, and agree they are very Siamese-like!

Dixie turned out to be an amazing dog, and we soon adopted a second Iggy, Whistle, from the same rescue group. No one told me, however, that the Iggy breed is quite difficult to house train, and for years we dealt with puddles throughout the house. While I may stink at preparing myself as an adopter, I am very good at finding animals with peeing issues.

Okay, enough dogs (and believe me, by this time we definitely had enough dogs); after all this time, I was still searching for a Beeky replacement. After a lot of auditions, I had finally found an excellent candidate. Two purebred cats, Alfonso and Blupert, came into the program when they had been abandoned by their owners at a boarding facility in Pennsylvania. Dropped off while the owners went on vacation, the owners never returned. (Wonder why?) After months of trying to contact them, the boarding kennel finally called us to see if we'd be willing to bring these two cats into our rescue program.

Now Siamese are often referred to by the shape of their heads. You have those that fall in the extreme category – the newer style breeder cats, or the Wedge Heads, with a very triangular shaped head – some people refer to these as the aliens of the Siamese world. They have their own fan club, and their personality really is quite different (read as much more intense) from the opposite end of the spectrum, known as the Applehead. Applehead Siamese are also known as the "old fashioned" Siamese. They have a rounder or more apple-shaped head, their body is stockier and their fur is often a thicker, more flannel-type of coat. Consequently, in general, their personality is also a bit less intense. In the middle, you'll find the Classic Siamese – a bit of both.

Wedge Heads (commonly referred to as Wedgies) come with their own set of medical and behavioral issues. The smaller, triangular-shaped head often results in a lot of dental crowding, and thus more frequent dental work is typically needed. Their sinus cavities are usually very narrow, and drainage between the eyes and the nose can be compromised. They have very long, thin bodies, whippy tails, and a very tight fur coat. And their behavior can be somewhat high strung - let's just say that Wedge Heads need an entirely different type of adopter than the Appleheads do.

Alfonso and Blupert fell into the extreme Wedge Head category, with Alfonso having a lot more issues than Blupert. Blupert was, well, a typical blue, and with apologies in advance to the blue point owners out there, my experience has been that in general, the blues are not known for being the brightest of lightbulbs. While they can be super nice, they are not the most robust in personality and tenacity. Based on what we often saw in the blue points that came through Rescue, we coined a term early on: the "Blue Wuss Syndrome." As expected, cats came into the program with all sorts of issues, but suffice it to say that the URI, or Upper Respiratory Infection, was one of the most common. Just like a terrible cold in humans, cats with URIs exhibit the same signs and symptoms: clogged noses, fevers, lethargy, general achiness. And just like with humans, it takes antibiotics to tackle any bacterial portion of the URI, and time and supportive care (syringe feeding, fluids, and anti-virals) to tackle the viral aspect. Many blue points, however, touched by the slightest bit of a URI, would immediately act as if the world had ended. You could just see them saying "I'm dying here, really, I'm on my last leg, and time is very short." All of the other Siamese points seemed to muddle through the URI without a lot of drama. Because of this tendency, whenever a Foster would report that their blue point foster cat was just not perking up, I would explain the Blue Wuss Syndrome to them, and tell them it was likely just a matter of time and supportive care. They needed to convince this drama king (or queen) of a cat that the world was not ending and that they needed to just buck up and get on with life. And so, with a lot of convincing, Blupert muddled through the initial URI, (although he continued throughout his life emanating general wussiness).

Alfonso

Alfonso, a seal point Wedgie, was actually in much worse physical shape than Blupert, but he had a determined spirit. His face was so triangular that his nictitating membranes (the third eyelid) covered over half his eyeballs on each side. This gave him a really funny looking face. The first vet who examined Alf, when noting his eyelids, his sinus issues, and his bloodwork, told me he would likely not last all that long. She thought perhaps he had Feline Infectious Peritonitis (FIP), a serious condition that at the time was often the go-to diagnosis when a cat was struggling, and everything else had been ruled out. At the very first vet visit Alf was such a mess that the vet, when checking his teeth, pulled out one of his canines with a gentle tug (it was hanging by a thread) as Alf stood there purring. While Alf was fine and barely noticed, I almost passed out in the examination room.

It wasn't long after Alf and Blupert had arrived at the Center that I fell for Alfonso. At last, my next soulmate cat. Since they came as a pair and were quite bonded to each other, we weren't going to separate them, so we brought them both over to the house to live with the rest of the crew. Blupert, whose nickname could have been Eeyore, was a bit of a bum. Alf, on the other hand, was quite the character. Due in part to his limited eyesight, Alf's navigation was not the best; I'm not sure he could even really tell what was going on most of the time. Coupled with his quite eccentric personality (and what we liked to call his pea brain), he had a repertoire of odd behaviors. Alf absolutely loved chicken of any kind, and one of his quirky habits was to run full tilt in circles round and round the kitchen island, then reverse direction, repeating the performance. He would do this any time he thought chicken was in his future, meowing loudly. This circling the island soon became known as Alf's Chicken Dance. This would later morph into the dance that was done by the volunteers at our annual awards event, but that's for another chapter. There was no doubt that Alf was the cat I was looking for when I started this whole thing – the Beeky replacement, my second soulmate cat. All of the other cats I had met and kept along the way were great, but I finally realized that it takes a very specific purrsonality to make it to soulmate status.

Not long after we had made an adoption commitment to keep these two, Alfonso earned the middle initial of P. Initially standing for Peabrain, he quickly became a Peebody. Most likely the reason that his owner had left them at the boarding kennel in Pennsylvania, Alf turned out to be quite the accomplished sprayer. There seemed to be no rhyme or reason to it; you could actually see a smile cross his face as he would back up to whatever he happened to be standing near, and let out a stream of urine. As annoying as this was, when watching the expression on his face as he wiggled his butt back and forth, it was hard not to crack a smile. By this time, we had committed: I was in love, and besides, with this new behavior Alf certainly was not adoptable by anyone else. A sanctuary placement wouldn't suit him due to his long, thin body type, as sanctuary candidates must have the body mass to tolerate the weather. He was here to stay.

While we had other cats over the years that weren't stellar in the litterbox, Alfonso P. Wallabee really made his mark, so to speak. We tried all the tricks in the book: calming medications (over the counter as well as various types of pharmaceuticals), pheromone plug-ins, a change in diet. We even tried diapering him (unlike his successor, stay tuned), he put up quite a battle, crying and chewing at it endlessly. Over the years that we had Alf, our home was modified to be the most waterproofed house you could possibly imagine. Darrell invented all sorts of protective coverings for just about everything. He lined the walls from the floor to about eighteen inches high with a type of waterproof plastic. The cabinets were coated with thick polyurethane; the flooring was resealed, and the furniture had sheets of a heavy vinyl-type material protecting anything accessible from the floor. Sounds lovely, right? We used to joke that if we ever had a flood inside the house, it would fill up just like a swimming pool.

After a few years, Blupert passed away due to a nasal carcinoma. Alf however, continued on for some years after that, becoming the Siamese Rescue mascot. Being completely toothless from the start, we never knew exactly how old he was, but he lived with us for nine happy (and wet) years before succumbing to a stroke. I was absolutely heartbroken at the loss but comforted by understanding that, with enough exposure, I would likely find another soulmate cat. Thousands of dollars later, after replacing all of the drywall that was damaged when the plastic panels were removed, we were back to a pee-free environment. Or so we thought.

Two soulmates almost in a row. How lucky is that? It was not long after Alfonso passed away that we were notified of a senior cat who had been turned into a high kill public shelter in New Jersey. The picture of him circulating the internet absolutely tore me in two – the saddest, most alarmed looking chocolate point male Wedge Head named Bibbles.

To top it off, he had been turned in to the shelter with a note that read "this is the best cat EVER." Suspicious, right? Who would turn in the best cat ever to a high kill public shelter? (There's always a catch.) Still, I could not get that picture out of my mind, and even though he was quite old, I knew that this cat had to come to the Center to audition for the role of my next soulmate kitty.

Transport was organized, and Bibbles arrived, as we expected, with a raging upper respiratory infection. Another Wedgie with that narrow nose, and a chocolate point (second to the blues in terms of their lack of tenacity), this cat was absolutely determined he was going to die. No matter what I did, or what I offered, he would not eat. Now, remember that cats, unlike dogs, cannot go very long without sustenance before their body starts breaking down the fat in the liver. By the time he finally ate on his own, Bibbles held the record for going the longest time of any cat we had ever had at the Center who refused to eat. When he finally decided life might just be worth living, it had been a hair-raising twenty-five days filled with subcutaneous fluids, syringe feeding, and coddling this cat to no end. I carried him everywhere, including for long walks outside. I sang to him, slept in the shelter with him, read him books - anything and everything I could think of to convince him to hang on.

When Bibbles eventually took that first bite and agreed to get back in the game, he was so bonded to me, and me to him, that there was no way he was going anywhere except over to the house. As our next family member, he integrated seamlessly with the four cats we had at the time. (What? Only four? Remember we adopted mostly the older cats, so many of the Geezers had, by now, crossed the Rainbow Bridge, as we say.) One of the big advantages we have found about adopting older cats is that they typically slot into existing home hierarchies without much fuss. Not worried about being the top cat, they are simply pleased to have a home.

Time went on, and Mr. Bibbles, as he was now known, felt better and stronger every day. He was so easygoing that he was happy to sleep with any of our animals, including Britainy, the female seal point Darrell had brought from Salt Lake, and Ziggy, our current Italian Greyhound. (All other dogs had passed on by this time.) He was, without a doubt, my next soulmate. Of course, the minute I said those words out loud, what happened? Yup, you guessed it. Mr. Bibbles put Alf to shame – he, too, made his mark as a superb sprayer. What in the world was it about me and cats who liked to spray everywhere?

Having just spent all that money replacing flooring, drywall, cabinets and just about everything else after our experience with Alf, we were determined not to go down that road again. It took a bit of convincing, but Mr. Bibbles learned to wear diapers. Foregoing the cat/dog specific diapers (which cost an arm and a leg and really didn't work very well) here I was, at fifty years of age, stocking up on Pampers. I always got a chuckle at the grocery store when the cashier asked about my grandbaby, and I told them the diapers were for my cat. I would take a size two diaper, measure an inch and a half down from the design around the waistband, and cut a diamond-shaped hole for the tail. Six times a day, including at least once in the middle of the night, Bibbles would get his diaper changed. Hey, it worked! There was no doubt at all that this cat became my very favorite cat *EVER*.

His daytime spot was just behind my computer monitor, where he'd watch me with the most loving eyes as I worked on the computer. Every evening he'd wait eagerly for it to be time for bed – the minute I headed up the stairs, he'd come trotting up as well. He slept in my arms every night – if I turned over, he'd get up, march across my face (usually with a full diaper, it was lovely) and settle back in my arms on the other side. Oh, how I miss you, Mr. Bibbles! And yes, our infamous "Diapering a Cat (Mr. Bibbles!)" video is on YouTube, complete with Bibbles complaining loudly.

To whoever turned this cat into that shelter, if you're reading this book, you were absolutely right, he was the best cat ever. While no one wants to live with a peeing cat, trust me, I get that, there are often options – for him it was diapers, and every dirty diaper was worth it. Regardless, your loss was my gain, that's for sure!

Mr. Bibbles

TO REHOME OR NOT, THAT IS THE QUESTION

I suspect many of us tend to condemn and criticize what other people choose to do concerning the rehoming of their animals. Certainly, with all of the social media avenues out there, the opportunities to pass judgment are endless. It is easy when reading about some scenario involving giving up an animal to think that we, personally, would have done something different. But it's important to remember that the old adage of "walking a mile in someone's shoes" should apply – we tend to make quick judgment calls, but one rarely knows the entire story behind the situation.

While it would be nice to insist that once you make a commitment to an animal, that commitment should be forever, sometimes it just isn't possible.

Life changes are often outside of our control, and there are instances when our hands may be forced concerning rehoming. Additionally, I truly feel that if the current situation for an animal is not a good one, for whatever reason, and the animal is unhappy, then the kindest thing may actually be to find an alternative situation that is better for the animal. You can do this the right way, or you can do it the wrong way, as we'll see in this chapter.

Animal Rescue, of course, involves a lot of rehoming, and no two situations are quite the same. There are legitimate situations, such as the death of the owner - these are easy to accept, as the cat must go somewhere. Then there are poor excuses. What we learned early on was not to waste time laying blame, but instead to use our energy to gather as much information as we could about the cat, in order to make a great placement the next time around. If the owner was unhappy, then the chances were very high that the cat was unhappy; in our opinion, removing the cat from that household and finding them a better situation made the most sense.

Remember Whitney? I stood in a room with a couple who had been married nine years: they were clearly very much in love. When they got married, the husband gave the wife a Siamese kitten as a wedding present; she had grown up with Siamese cats and absolutely adored them. Fast forward nine years. They both loved the cat; Whitney had been an only cat and as such was "their treasured child."

Their life had revolved around this lovely blue point girl. After about four years of marriage, they tried to start a family. What followed over the next few years was the frustrating, emotional rollercoaster of trying to get pregnant. Finally, they succeeded. A baby girl joined their family – they were ecstatic. And then the bad news. The infant was deathly allergic to many things, but one of the primary culprits? Animal dander.

They did what they could, visiting numerous doctors; despite all of their best efforts, their little girl was repeatedly hospitalized. So there they stood in our living room, the wife holding Whitney tightly in her arms. Both of them had tears streaming down their face (as did I). They had exhausted the few family and friend possibilities that existed; their only option was to rehome her. While this was heartbreaking for everyone, Whitney went on to live a very happy life in her new home. Despite having to give her up, the ending was a good one.

Scenario number two: A sixty-five-year-old woman just retired from her very stressful job. Some years ago, when she was deeply mired in the daily unhappiness at work, she got a kitten to give herself something to look forward to when she went home. Now, rid of the hateful boss, the dreadful commute and the daily verbal abuse, she felt free and wanted to travel the world. She dropped her cat off without a second glance at an overcrowded public shelter. If the cat was lucky, it got adopted or picked up by a rescue group, but more likely than not, if it was frightened, older, didn't "show" well, or had any health or behavior issues, she may well have condemned that cat to death. Not only did this lady not plan ahead when she first got the kitten, but she didn't look for alternatives when she decided to rehome it. This was most likely not a good ending for the cat.

Another very common situation is the aging up of the owner. An eighty-year-old man, who had one grown daughter, lived with his friend, a twelve-year-old male Siamese seal point. They were joined at the hip. Except, when he fell and broke that hip, he went first into extended rehab and from there to a nursing home that didn't allow pets, his only option. His daughter's job involved constant travel, so she was unable to take his cat, and they could find no one else who could. If the cat was lucky, it got into a Rescue program, but many of these cats end up in the overcrowded public shelters where the chances of adoption may be slim.

The stories are endless. Each story, in itself, has countless manifestations with a zillion different extenuating circumstances. Sometimes rehoming is a justified step; other times it is not. While many of us may dissect each and every scenario, analyzing the choices made, this is only helpful in that we can come away with some tenets that all pet owners should consider in advance. By understanding these tenets, perhaps we can avoid a situation where we need to rehome a pet.

Let's start by backing up, rewinding to the point in time before adding a new pet. There are several things to be considered first. Time and money are two of the basics. It will take a commitment of time for a new pet to adjust to a new environment, and there will be some costs involved (vet visits for example). Don't take on a new pet if either your time or your budget are already stretched to the limit. If time and funds are available, the second thing to think about is personality matching: you want to make sure there is a match of animal to person, animal to household, and animal to other animals. Just like people, not every cat is going to like every other cat. Finally, taking on an animal does mean, I believe, taking on the responsibility of making sure the animal is safe for life (be it with you or with someone else). It's not just the here and now of acquiring a pet; it's looking into the future as well.

Unforeseen circumstances happen every day. The number of cats that come into Rescue when something unexpected happens to the owner is amazing. It is really important to have a plan for the future should your pet need help. I realize many people are so focused on making it through the present that it's difficult to think about the future. However, if you don't put a plan in place, the animal(s) may well end up in a very unfortunate situation at some point in time. Just as you should plan for your assets to be distributed somewhere when the time comes, you should have a plan for your pets to go somewhere. Assign a family member or good friend to take on the responsibility of the animal should something happen to you: they don't necessarily have to keep the animal, but they do accept responsibility to ensure that if the pet must be rehomed, it is done safely and responsibly. At the same time, don't tempt the fates. If you are sixty-five years of age or older, you had better be thinking about the future very carefully if you're adding a young animal to your household. That animal might just live to be fifteen or twenty years old. While we'd all like to think we'll be spring chickens at the age of eighty, many of us won't. We may be using a walker, in a wheelchair, in a nursing home, or living in some such situation that doesn't allow us to have a pet.

Over the years of Siamese Rescue, one of our commitments has always been to take back (or help to place) any alumnae of our program. The numbers were surprising – one in ten of the cats we placed needed us at some point again in the future, and the majority of the time, it was because of something unforeseen. Please plan for your pet's future, even if you don't plan for your own.

As far as adding new pets goes, spending time up front to make sure the animal you may adopt is actually going to work for your household is key. Over time, shelters and rescues have gotten much better with their matchmaking process, but it wasn't always so. I remember when my daughter was small, walking into a public shelter and walking out the same day with a puppy. (Every little girl needs a puppy, despite the fact we already had four dogs in the home.) Never once was I quizzed as to whether I had ample room for the puppy, whether I was ready for that puppy to grow into a 150-pound clumsy dog, what other animals would be affected, and so forth. Yes, we kept Pepper her entire life, but had someone spent the time with me discussing the ramifications of adopting a soon-to-be overwhelming dog for a small five-year-old girl, I might have given it more serious thought.

Being an internet-based placement agency necessitates doing a lot of in-depth screening up front, as more often than not we don't get to physically meet our adopters. Our screening procedures are not only designed to make sure the home is a good one but more importantly, to find out about the person and the environment so that we can work our matchmaking magic. While not everyone is keen on the multitude of questions we ask, those who adopt from us are almost always delighted in the end.

Choosing the right cat can take a bit of work. In general, there is quite a difference between the male and the female Siamese personality – something I suspect is true in many breeds. Male cats are often the lovers. They are more likely to be the ones you would hold upside down like a baby, snuggle in your arms in bed, and carry around with you. Females tend to be smarter – they are the ones to discuss world affairs with you, to be adoring but on their own terms, and to have moments of moodiness.

With Siamese, there are also some generalizations we can make based on their coloring. Seal points tend to be the "most Siamese," often exhibiting that keen intelligence, sensitivity and demanding nature. While some would say that tortie points aren't really Siamese, we see many a tortie point that behaves like a seal female in disguise (torties are always females, just as calicos are). Chocolates are often softer, gentler seals in their personality. Blues, as previously discussed, sometimes score a little lower on the intelligence scale and are often "blue wusses." Lilacs, and we see very few of these, are often very sedate with a soft personality. Flames or red points (some will argue that these are orange tabbies with blue eyes) are usually males and have a reputation for being the most laid back, easy going, happy-go-lucky of them all. Lynxes (some striping evident) are usually a blend of Siamese plus something else and thus tend to have more of a Domestic Shorthair personality. Snowshoes (for our purposes, any point with some white on them, particularly on their paws) are often playful, opinionated, and known to be a handful at times.

In Siamese Rescue, Fosters would take into account these generalizations, any history that came with the cat, and the observations made while in foster care, and come up with the type of home best suited for the cat. Interviewers would gather information about the applicant's desires, their home, and any existing pets, and come up with the type of cat best suited for that home. And then

Foster plus Interviewer plus applicant (plus myself as overseer) would confer on the potential matches.

Careful matchmaking is, of course, not one hundred percent. Sometimes, despite our best efforts, discord happens. When that occurs, how does one know when rehoming is justified? Just like many things, it often comes down to how hard and how long one has tried to allow things to work out.

Let's say you have a thriving household with a cat and a dog, and you add one more. You have already determined you have the time, the finances, and the patience to add a new family member. You do a slow and careful introduction, isolating the new family member first. Not only do you want to give the new family pet a chance to decompress, but you want to allow all existing family members to get used to the idea. This does not happen overnight – suggested isolation time is a minimum of two weeks. If you are having difficulty with integration, you consult experts – researching things to try, talking with your vet and/or finding an animal behaviorist - investing in whatever it takes to work towards happy animals.

Well, what if you have spent several months trying all of those things, and still have not reached a happy and stable situation? Is keeping the new animal the right thing to do? The first question to be sure to ask yourself: who is unhappy? Is it you, because the animal is disrupting your status quo, or is it the animal? If it's just you, then the argument that "you took on the pet, you should now put up with any inconveniences," may be a valid one. If it's the animal that is unhappy because of a situation that can't be changed, is there a better solution somewhere else, or are you providing the best that is possible for this particular animal? White picket fences rarely exist for people, let alone for animals. Look at the situation carefully: is the current set-up the best one available? Sometimes the best we can offer also happens to be the best that's out there for the animal. Other times, finding a better situation, if it exists, may be the way to go.

Let's take a fourteen-year-old cat who, because of previous abuse, can be somewhat aggressive. Let's call her Teyla (and yes, she was one of our cats). She doesn't particularly like other cats, although she can tolerate them if they leave her alone. Teyla's ideal situation would be a home as the only cat, where there was one experienced cat owner who had nothing else to do but work with her. Does that home really exist? It's unlikely for a fourteen-year-old, and even if the cat was much younger, it's tough finding this type of adopter. The best we are likely to find for this gal is a situation where she can live out her life without being bothered by other cats, yet still, get a little personal attention. This may mean she lives her last few years in a section of a house, away from other cats, with part-time attention. The world is not perfect, and sometimes the best one can do is the best there is.

If and when one decides that rehoming is the

best option for the animal, then doing it responsibly, by making an effort and taking the time to find a different situation that works in the animal's best interest, is a necessity. Turning the animal outdoors to fend for themselves is not a good option; there are too many dangers. Likewise, turning the animal into a shelter forced to euthanize due to lack of space (owner surrenders can be the first to go) is also not the answer. If you committed to the animal in the first place, incorporated into that commitment is making sure the animal continues to be safe, even if it doesn't happen to be with you.

Over the years, both Darrell and I rehomed animals, at one point irresponsibly (me), at other times responsibly (both of us). The irresponsible approach remains a very painful memory. The responsible approach? Those animals were much happier in a situation that was better suited to them.

As mentioned previously, Darrell decided upon moving to Virginia, in the best interest of two of his cats, that rehoming was the best thing for them. They had been unhappy in a multi-cat household; they were beating up the other cats; the spray wars were overwhelming. They went on to live much happier lives in their new home as the only two cats, not having to compete with so many others for attention. I, too, was faced with rehoming on two different occasions – the first time I did it the wrong way, the second time I was much better at it.

As you may recall, when we moved to the house

we're currently in, we had three dogs – soon to increase to five. We had the Shepherd mix, named Scout; we had a Collie mix, named Solomon, and we had a Terrier mix, named Benji. We had several indoor cats, plus the two cats we were still letting outdoors, Kipper and Opie; they would wander the six acres during the day, coming back inside each evening.

The back of our property was an acre of land that was fenced, providing a lovely area for the dogs to romp and play and remain outside unsupervised for a length of time, as needed. They had several dog houses and were perfectly delighted to spend time lounging in the Virginia sunshine. It was mid-afternoon when I heard quite the commotion in the back yard - lots of barking and snapping. Running outside, I saw Opie streaking across the back yard, the dogs in close pursuit. On a day-to-day basis, all of the dogs and cats lived in the home and got along marvelously – there were no conflicts whatsoever. That having been said, in the past on more than one occasion, Solomon had shown a slight bit of aggression with several of my daughter's friends. No one was bitten or anything, and at the time I chalked it up to his protecting my daughter when the kids were roughhousing. As I watched Solomon leading the pack in hot pursuit of Opie, it was obvious to me that if Solomon were to catch Opie, he would have killed him. There was nothing playful about what I was witnessing. I could just tell by Solomon's demeanor, as I watched Opie race for his life.

Luckily, Opie reached the deck and leaped over the railing, dashing through the door to the inside where I was standing, and was safe. Solomon came to a screeching halt, and it took a few minutes for him to wind down – you could literally see the pack mentality of "attack to kill" in his eyes. And I was simply pushed over the edge. The possibility of what almost happened to Opie was just too much – and without a second thought, I put Solomon in the car and drove him to the public shelter.

Now, even years later, I still cringe at what I did. My heart hurts, for I know I sentenced that dog to death. I knew nothing about public shelters at the time, let alone about the overpopulation of animals and the overcrowding that is rampant in those shelters. It was, without a doubt, one of the biggest mistakes I have made in my life. I just didn't know any better.

As I indicated earlier, we are all going to make mistakes. As long as we can turn those mistakes into future positive actions, for oneself and for others, then some good can be found.

My hope is, throughout this book, readers will learn from my mistakes.

By the time Rescue officially opened its doors, I understood a lot more about animal welfare. As the number of cats in our home slowly but continually increased (input did not equal output at this point), my personal (original) cats were not all that happy about these changes. This was particularly true of Suki, a seal point kitten that I purchased shortly after losing our Siamese blue point Triscuit. I made a very inaccurate (but common) assumption: if I got a cat as a kitten, I would be able to mold her personality into the cat I wanted. I knew little about genetics versus environment with respect to cats; I certainly had yet to learn about seal point divas. Surely, if I carried her around in my pocket all the time; if I showered her with non-stop love and attention, she'd turn into the cat I wanted, and become my soulmate. What I found instead was that while my actions would definitely impact her behaviors, much of her personality was already set. As it turned out, I had a very independent seal point female that was both quite headstrong and quite smart. If I had known about the difference between males and females, I would have chosen a male. If I had known that seal females were independent and often didn't like to share, I might not have chosen a seal.

Suki, the most perfect example of a seal point diva, was absolutely not receptive to having a parade of visiting cats come through the house. She quickly took it upon herself to make her opinion known by peeing on every piece of cat bedding she could find. As time went on, and more and more cats left their scent in our home, she got more and more agitated, peeing on the furniture, the floors, just about everywhere except the litterbox. It got so bad that at one point I started having to crate her when I couldn't watch her. I found myself faced with quite a dilemma – clearly, Suki had not asked to be put in this situation, and she was obviously unhappy with the starting up of the Rescue organization. To back out of the Rescue at this point just wasn't something I felt was the right thing to do. To have a cat peeing everywhere was not going to work, either for me or for all of the rescued cats coming through the house. The more she peed, the more the other cats would start peeing. And to keep her caged most of the time was no life for her.

One afternoon I was introducing an adopter to the various cats I had for adoption. The adopter had a good history with Siamese, but currently had no cats, and was looking for a female who was smart, outgoing, and who could travel with her in her retirement. I introduced her to this one and that one, but no cat seemed to be quite the right match. As we sat on the floor discussing what type of lifestyle she had and what she was looking for, a thought occurred to me, although it was a difficult one to swallow. Seeing the conflict on my face, she asked me what was up. Still unsure as to how to handle my difficult situation, I explained the trouble I was having with Suki. The more I told her about Suki, the more she looked intrigued. I brought the adopter upstairs to where I had Suki crated for the day in my bedroom. Sitting on the floor, I let her out, and Suki, giving the adopter a very thorough once over, climbed into her lap. There was, without a doubt, a connection there, and both adopter and Suki spent the next fifteen minutes making friends. Despite everything I had been brought up to believe about committing to a pet for life, the situation that was best for Suki was sitting right in front of me. And so, with a lot of tears and a somewhat heavy heart, I agreed to adopt Suki out to this adopter.

Out of all the lessons I've learned with Rescue, this was one of the most valuable. It should be about the animals, not about the humans. What we want, or need, is not always what's best for the animal.

Now a lot of people will argue that an animal that has been rehomed will be absolutely devastated. Yes, some will; look at Mr. Bibbles. He was ever so sad, making it really difficult to pull him through. The older the cat, the harder it can be for the animal. The tougher the environment they go into (remember, he went into a high kill public shelter) the more traumatic it is for them. But that having been said, and trust me, we did this for over twenty years and placed over 12,000 cats; the majority of the cats are incredibly resilient. Give them the right situation – despite it being a new environment – if it's loving, kind, compassionate, and meeting the needs of the cat, the cat can adjust remarkably well. We have to be careful not to over-impose our human emotions onto animals because we're not the same species. We may, as humans, be heartbroken at the loss of a family member, and we may never quite recover. Animals tend to be much better than we are at change.

Please understand, I am by no means advocating the rehoming of animals. I absolutely believe that a) careful thought should be given prior to adoption, including considering a plan for the future, and b) once you've committed to an animal coming into the home, every effort should be made to accommodate that animal's needs so that they can be happy in the house. I also realize that it can be r*eally* tough to find alternative situations for animals – there are so many animals out there without a home already. But if the circumstances cannot be adjusted so that the animal is happy, *and* an alternative beneficial situation can be found, then responsible rehoming may, in some instances, be justified.

For Suki, she went on to live fifteen wonderful years with this adopter. They traveled all over the United States in an RV; I got constant updates with pictures of Suki looking as content as could be. There was no doubt she was much happier than she would have been dealing with all of the cats in Rescue. A very tough decision for me to make, but it was without a doubt the right decision for Suki.

Suki

OH, POOP, SHE'S HERE TO STAY!

As mentioned previously, one of the early policies we instituted was to always accept back, or if there was no way to do that, at least help to rehome, any alumnae of our program that needed us. One of every ten cats we placed would need our help again at some point in the future, and sometimes more than once.

Whenever we did have a cat returned to the program, we would analyze the reasons for the placement failure and then look to see if we could have foreseen the reason the placement didn't work. We classified our returns as either "preventable" or "non-preventable" with each of these categories having sub-categories. For example, non-preventable might include loss of home, job transfer overseas, or death of owner - the type of things that no one could have predicted, as life threw a curve ball into the mix. As time went on and we got better, almost all of our returns were non-preventable. Kudos to our amazing Interviewers and Fosters for this.

One of the non-preventable situations that occurred, despite all of our matchmaking, was when the cat just didn't like the adopter. While some of our adopters got to meet the cats first (if, for example, they lived close enough to the Foster who was housing the cat they were interested in), the majority did not. Being internet-based, a large number of our adoptions were done without physical interaction between the cat and the person. After sharing a lot of pictures, videos, and discussions, a match was made. With the exchange of so much information, we would feel relatively confident that the person liked the cat, however, every so often, the cat didn't like the person. Luckily this "non-preventable" return didn't happen much – we have such a group of wonderful (and highly likable) adopters!

When we did get to meet the adopter first, and the cat disliked the adopter, we were able to intervene. Talk about a tricky conversation to have with a potential adopter when, as the cat's advocate, we had to explain that the cat they wanted just didn't like them! We once had a seal point Wedgie (Toko) who was very popular; he had a long list of interested applicants. When his first in line came to visit, he turned his back on her, wanting to have absolutely nothing to do with the family. After watching him interact with visitors and volunteers, it was clear he preferred tall blondes. Fortunately, in his case, we discovered this before he went home.

Returns that fell into the "preventable" category helped us define our placement guidelines, as over time we learned what did and didn't work in our matchmaking. We found that two female Siamese, particularly if they were seal points and close in age, were unlikely to get along. A very forward or bully-type cat wasn't going to mesh with a shy victim-type kitty. A super playful kitten would often push an elderly geezer over the edge with its constant demand for interaction.

Matching a cat to a person who had no experience with Siamese was also quite tricky, particularly if we made the match online. We learned quickly that the personality of the person and that of the cat needed to be similar. Placing a very extroverted cat with a shyer, introverted person was often a recipe for a return. (I once had a lovely adopter call me after adopting her first Siamese seal point female. "This gal won't get off my lap," she said, "and I'm afraid that if I get up, I will make her mad.")

The good news was that with almost every single return, we would have much more in-depth information about the cat, for we'd now know what the cat was like in the home setting, versus in the rescue program. We were, therefore, able to make a much better match the second time around. Through the years we only had four cats (out of 12,000) that were returned more than three times. Two we placed in the sanctuary, and two were successful in a home on their fourth try. Once in a great while, we'd have a return that was not placeable because of a behavior or personality issue, and they were not suited to sanctuary living. These cats would then become what we would term a Center Resident.

Which brings us to Dinky.

Dinky became a Center Resident when, after being returned to us, we realized she was unadoptable due to her medical issues. As mentioned previously, a few of the unadoptable cats were placed in a sanctuary, but Dinky's size and her issues disqualified her from being a good candidate. Over time, she became a favorite challenge and was loved by everyone, living her life out in Group Living at the Center.

Dinky was a tiny five-pound seal point snowshoe

who was originally turned over to us when she had been left at a vet's office by an owner who no longer wanted her. She had no tail at all (previously amputated at some point, was our guess, although it's possible she could have been born that way) and came into our program where she stayed for a number of months before being adopted by a single lady with no other pets. During the time she was with us, there were no apparent issues other than a very typical seal snowshoe personality – an opinionated female who didn't like to be told what to do. About a year post adoption she was returned to us when she was having repeated constipation issues: unable to pass stool, so constipated that she would vomit, repeatedly needing to visit the vet for an enema. After months of struggling, the owner was no longer able to manage the situation, and Dinky came back to us here at the Center.

Sure enough, Dinky was one easily constipated kitty. We tried lots of different foods: wet, dry, even a raw diet. We made sure we always had water fountains going, and we administered subcutaneous fluids daily to help her hydration status. Back and forth to our vet, we tried various medications – those designed to increase fiber, those designed to relax the gut, those designed to stimulate the colon, those that were to soften the stool. I even took to putting her in a carrier and driving her up and down the road, which initially worked, to get her to pass stool.

Diagnosed with megacolon, where a portion of

the colon becomes so stretched and diseased from constant constipation that it "stores" stool rather than allowing it to pass, things were not getting any easier for poor Dinky. Despite all of the things we tried, she still required enemas about once a week. While, at first, I would run her into the vet for the enema, pretty soon I had not only mastered giving an enema but could do it one-handed. (Oh, the things this job has allowed me to add to my resume.) Dinky, by this point, was not the most cooperative for enemas, so with my left hand I would scruff her, and with my right hand, administer. You can certainly guess why she earned the nickname Stinky Dinky.

As the months went by, things got harder and harder for Dinky (pun intended). Things were just going downhill. She was clearly not adoptable, we knew that, but at this point in time, what was her quality of life like? What was the kindest thing to do? While we consider ourselves a "no-kill facility," one has to make exceptions for cats that are so medically involved, they are suffering. We certainly didn't want to keep a cat going when their quality of life was so poor. Enduring enema after enema was no way to live.

Visiting our vet yet again to discuss if there were any options left to us, Dr. R felt that the only thing left to do was to try resecting the colon. This involved opening her up, trying to determine what part of the colon was diseased, removing what needed to be removed, and then re-suturing the colon back together. He wasn't sure whether this type of surgery would fix her problem, but he was willing to try to see if it would help her situation. Given that the alternative was not a good one, we opted to let Dr. R try his best.

The surgery was completed, and Dinky came back to the Center to recover. Sure enough, Dinky could now pass stool with the best of them. As a matter of fact, she would pass stool whenever and wherever the urge hit. We had gone from the rare poop occasion to the opposite end of the spectrum: constant poo instances that landed everywhere in the Center one could imagine. Dinky was a real Sky Meezer (always climbing up high), and one had to be very careful pulling anything down off from a shelf, as one never knew what else might come tumbling down. She absolutely loved the amazing "Millie Beds" made by our talented Crafters; we'd always find "Dinky Doodles" in the bed creases. While Dinky would go on to eat, drink and eliminate happily ever after, she was still not adoptable. Even though she was one messy kitty, we all loved her dearly. We even had buttons made up for the weekend volunteers that read "I cleaned Dinky's cage."

And what could we do to thank Dr. R for all his patience with us throughout this process, his efforts to help Dinky multiple times over the months before surgery, as well as the surgery itself? Why, that very first stool she passed, I found the perfect sized gift box, laid it neatly between some tissue paper and wrapped it up, and presented it to him as a thank you gift.

Dinky was one of several cases that really challenged our vets. One of the things we learned from her situation was to always inquire about litterbox behavior when we evaluated a cat without a tail. In Dinky's case, it was possible that the tail had been amputated too close to the rectum, damaging some of the sphincter muscles.

We were so lucky to have so many great vets to work with over the years, something I felt pretty well qualified to judge, for, as Director, I was charged with approving the vet work on all of the cats coming through our program. This was not only for the hundreds of cats that came through the Center and saw our local vets but all the cats in the foster homes (seventy-five foster homes at one time in sixteen different states). This meant that between Darrell and I, we worked directly with some 200 different vets over the years. And just like any profession, not all vets are created equally.

There was the old country vet in Tennessee who, when I questioned him on whether he meant 'FIV' or 'FIP' on a cat's paperwork, he replied "Not really sure, those two always confuse me." (Really? They are two completely different feline diseases.) There was the vet in Virginia who was supposed to spay one of our cats and instead declawed it by mistake. And while I understand you just can't expect the cost of living to be even close to similar when comparing rural Kentucky with Boston, it was always hard to swallow that the very same rabies vaccine from the very same manufacturer costs $3.00 in Kentucky and $43 in Boston (no vet visits included).

Of course, the majority of the vets we worked with were wonderful. There was Dr. B, who, while I realize it's a somewhat unfortunate reputation to have, was, without a doubt, the absolute best in her kindness and gentleness when it came to euthanasia. There was Dr. N, who, when we began the organization, donated older medical equipment and supplies to help. There is, of course, Dr. R, who is always ready to try something new, Dr. AM and Dr. D, who both became good friends as well as being fantastic vets, and a slew of other vets who helped in so many ways. We had vets who traveled to our Spring Training Event to present workshops, worked hand in hand with our Fosters over the years to diagnose and treat within our Rescue budget, provided Fosters with, in many cases, 24/7 advice via text or email, and discounted their services to help the cats. In exchange, we provided many of our vets with some interesting challenges and learning opportunities.

One such challenge was a fluffier seal point gal named Jasmine. Another cat from the Fairfax hoarding case, she came into the program at a year or so of age with a slight head tilt. Additionally, she was kind of skitzy on the socialization scale. She had a lovable expression and a deep-seated "I want to be a good cat if only I knew how" look in her eyes. The problem was that she was really klutzy – she'd list to one side, fall over on occasion, and every so often demonstrate a set of crazy dance steps that involved a lot of circle twirling followed by a collapse. A few minutes later she'd be back to normal, albeit with a confused look in her eyes.

Because of the hoarding situation that she came from, we realized this could have been due to all sorts of things; those cats were in horrendous shape. Ear issues were ruled out; bloodwork was run – nothing was obvious. Epilepsy was considered and fit the seizure part of her behavior, but at other times there would be extended periods where she would cavort like a drunken sailor. While we didn't go the MRI route, we did all the diagnostics we could afford and found very little to go on. She seemed, over a period of several months, to slowly get worse. Eventually, we ended up with a cat whose tilted head and lopsided tumbles made it close to impossible for her to manage both the food bowl and the litterbox.

The vet we used at the time was just wonderful – Dr. N – she would always help in any way she could, including taking the more difficult cases home with her to observe for a few days to determine the best course of action. This was so appreciated because there was only so much she could see within our thirty-minute vet visit. She offered to do this with Jasmine; for at this point we were keeping her caged all the time. When she had these "episodes", she would get so panicked that her safety became an issue, as she flailed around the room.

One of the internal practices we instituted early on in Rescue was to have the Foster sign an Adoption Agreement if any cat was likely to be a hospice cat, i.e., either we weren't going to adopt them out, or we thought that their end was near. This way, in theory, that cat belonged to someone and officially had a home before they passed away. This was one of many things we did to make ourselves feel better (the cat likely knew no difference). As we were learning, Rescue wasn't just about the cats.

After several overnights with Dr. N, we sat down to confer on what to do. Things had just gotten worse and worse for Jasmine, and neither of us could come up with ideas on the cause or the treatment. Maybe a brain tumor, maybe some kind of progressive inner ear issue, but regardless (and even if we had been able to do advanced diagnostics) the outcome didn't look to be a good one. While we were willing to keep trying, this was another situation where we had to question what her quality of life was like. The dreaded "E" needed to be considered. Being one of our very early cats and not yet having had to face this decision with any of the rescued cats, I was dragging my feet. I just didn't want to go down that road. It was decided I would bring Jasmine back home, give it another night or two, discuss it with the Board of Directors, and then get back to Dr. N.

When we got home, I set Jasmine up in a small dog crate on our dining table where I could carefully monitor her food and water intake, as well as her behavior. She had obviously gone downhill over the months we had her, and lay, tilted head and all, in her cage. That night, I sat down at the table with her, feeling very down and depressed. I must have sat there for several hours, feeding her little table scraps, talking with her, trying so hard to make it not so. As I got ready for bed, I finally admitted to myself that her quality of life was really very poor. I knew that I needed to make that awful decision the next morning, and I went ahead and signed that adoption agreement.

The next day I woke with that heavy, sad lump in my stomach that comes when it's time to say goodbye. The plan was for both Kevin and I to drive her over to the vets, then leave her body for cremation, returning at a later time to bring her ashes back for burial in the garden. Needless to say, we were both dreading the whole thing. As we came downstairs for our morning coffee, I heard Jasmine chirping at us. As I approached the cage, she straightened up, still wobbly but with a determined look on her face. As if to make a point, Jasmine gave me a "where is my breakfast" look, and then managed a visit to her food bowl. After a few crunchies, she looked at me expectantly, pawing at the cage door. Dubiously, I pulled her from the cage and put her on the floor, where she proceeded to rub against my legs, grinning with that huge Cheshire Cat grin. Jasmine was clearly showing me who won *that* adoption contest. You see, my cat collecting was not all my fault!

Jasmine went on to live another 11 years (yes, with us, what a surprise). About once a year she would have a seizure of some sort that would last maybe three or four minutes. By the time we would get her to the vet, she would have recovered, and nothing could be found. It was the strangest thing. No diagnosis was ever given, but she was a lovely cat who clearly outsmarted her adopters.

Jasmine

I'M OUTTA HERE!

By now you know we made some stupid, funny, and sometimes awful mistakes. As I keep saying, what was most important is that we learned something from those mistakes, and in our case, adjusted the way we did things so we could avoid them in the future. Our organization – all our policies and practices – went through a great deal of restructuring, changes, and adjustments (no, not just because we made so many mistakes). (Okay, well maybe a little.) The implementation of a post-adoption phone call came from one such horrible lesson.

Nibby Nose was a seal point female that came into our program from an owner who could no longer keep her – the owner was moving into a nursing home and couldn't bring her cat. Nibby had been a fairly healthy cat her whole life but was known to be a somewhat picky eater. Unfortunately, by the time we got her, the owner was unable to share any information about what did and didn't work with her as far as food goes, so we had to start from scratch. We always keep a wide variety of foods at the Center, so we started with our routine food trials – try the good stuff first, if that doesn't work move on to the middle of the road foods, if that doesn't work, then go for the junk foods. Continue to vary kibble sizes in the dry foods, in case the cat prefer, for example, round kibbles over star-shaped kibbles. Vary the textures of the wet foods, chunky versus slivers versus pate, and of course, try all of the flavors in each texture. Most of the time, we had no history, so we just had to try it all.

Additionally, it was not unusual to have an Owner Give-up be very depressed upon arrival in Rescue – it is often their first-ever shelter experience. They are caged, so we can observe their input and output; they are depressed at the change of environment, and they are taken aback by the smells of so many other cats. It's not surprising that it's a struggle to keep many of these cats going. Even though we worked quickly to integrate them into the population, allowing them free roam as soon as possible, there is almost always a period of withdrawal where the cats can shut down. Nibby Nose was no exception; the fact that she was a picky eater to start with didn't help. It turned out to be quite the challenge to find something she would eat.

If we strike out with cat food options, we move on to people food – scrambled eggs, shaved turkey, cooked hamburger, boiled chicken – because one never knows what a cat may have been fed, especially if they lived with an elderly owner. If we're not having any luck at this point, we'll add in an appetite stimulant, and if that still doesn't work, we'll syringe feed. Faced with a wide enough variety of foods, lots and lots of cuddling time, some subcutaneous fluids to keep their hydration going, and something to stimulate their appetite, the cats typically pull through, finally realizing that the world is not over and they are going to be alright.

The conundrum comes, of course, when we're forced to keep a cat caged, so we can observe their intake, yet at the same time, we know that the cage is actually contributing to their issues. Nibby Nose nibbled, but not a lot; she was so very sad at losing her home and did not want to perk up, no matter how many things I tried. I finally decided that perhaps she just needed to go to a home environment, that just maybe, in a situation that mimicked the one she had been in, she would perk up and get back to her previous eating habits.

Finding a home wasn't terribly difficult – she was beautiful, not too old, and by all appearances seemed to be quite healthy. A young lady from a nearby town came along; this would be her first cat ever, and it seemed to be the perfect situation for Nibby Nose. I sent her with some of the food that she had been nibbling on, as well as a variety of other foods to offer. Off the two of them went, and at this point, I made an enormous mistake. As busy as I was with the Rescue, I figured that if there were an issue, I would hear from the adopter. There is no doubt that I didn't give the two of them the follow-up that they deserved.

About ten days later, sure enough, I did hear from the adopter. Nibby hadn't been eating, she said. I asked for details, and as it turned out, Nibby Nose had been hiding under the couch since that very first day at home. The new owner had been putting down food and water near the sofa, but nothing had been disappearing. I asked whether there had been any activity in the litterbox; she remarked that she hadn't noticed any. At this point, extremely alarmed that not only was Nibby still hiding, but didn't seem to be eating anything, I asked her to pull her out from under the couch and take her to the local vet as quickly as possible. The adopter did as she was told, heading immediately to the vet. Meantime, I contacted the vet directly to explain the situation and to ask for an update as soon as possible.

Unfortunately, the vet called to tell me that Nibby Nose could not be saved. With minimal water or food intake in those ten days, her organs had already begun to shut down, and she had to be put to sleep. Needless to say, the owner was devastated – she had never realized that cats could just starve themselves if they were sad or frightened enough. She figured that when she got hungry enough, she would eat. There is no doubt that I had not done my due diligence. I should have explained to her, in detail, how critical it was that she pay close attention to what Nibby consumed.

I should have told her that she should carefully watch to see what was produced in the litterbox, for no activity in the box would mean that no food intake was happening. I was absolutely sick to my stomach, and it still brings tears to my eyes when I write this. I had not only let down this lovely cat but also failed miserably with this poor young lady who was so traumatized by this experience, she gave up on the idea of cat ownership altogether.

As hard as it was to admit that my failure had resulted in the unnecessary death of this kitty, I needed to find some way to make good from the bad – we had to make sure that this scenario would *never* happen again. We immediately instituted a third day, post-adoption, follow-up phone call with every adopter from that point forward. During this phone call, it was the Interviewer's responsibility to verify that the adopted cat was eating, drinking and using the litterbox, and to remind the adopter to call if they had any concerns. Additionally, we amended our Adoption Agreement to require a post-adoption vet visit. The notes that the Interviewer made were added as a permanent section of the cat's file, and as such, were appropriately named Nibby Notes.

Thanks to those changes, we've never had that issue occur again. The Nibby Notes have, however, given us some unexpected feedback at times.

About five years into Rescue we were no longer getting many requests from the shelters close to the Center – the Siamese that they got, they were able to place. The majority of the cats that ended up at the Center came from the surrounding urban areas – Fairfax, Virginia Beach, Richmond, and Baltimore. All are large shelters, serving a large population and therefore see quite a few Siamese. When the local shelters did call, we always felt that we should go the extra mile to help, as any neighbor should. So regardless of how much (or how little) the cat looked like a Siamese, we would typically accept the cat into our program, as long as it was super friendly.

Sturgeon was one such cat. Yes, I know, you are cringing at that name – but bear with me. When a cat comes in with a name given by their owner, we typically try to keep it – our thinking being that the cat has lost everything – their owner, their home, usually all their belongings. The name is the only thing they have left and most of the older cats know their names. So, while I thought it was an awful name, I stuck with it.

Sturgeon was a female tortie-calico mix with blue eyes. I can't say she was the prettiest of cats. She had been turned in to the shelter by her owner for reason #42 (no idea which one it was, shelters and rescues have heard them all). Once again, this was before the Center was built; Sturgeon was assigned the master bathroom as her isolation area (that would be the one hubby and I were using). Kevin was, once again, demonstrating his endless patience and good sportsmanship as, one weekend when home, going about his evening bathroom duties, he had to work around this overly friendly and outgoing gal. "Is this really a Siamese?" I remember him asking me. I heard the tub running, then all was silent for about ten minutes when all of a sudden there was a loud scream. Racing upstairs - I can't even begin to imagine what has happened – I threw open the door. There sat Kevin, in the tub, with Sturgeon, fully immersed alongside him, and looking *completely happy*. (Sturgeon, that was. Kevin, not so much.) Yes, Sturgeon had jumped into the tub, with Kevin, and was extremely pleased with herself.

Okay, so maybe this was a clue as to why she had been named Sturgeon?

Not long after that, despite her non-Siamese attire, she got adopted by a lovely lady who lived not too far from here. Not put off by her looks, the adopter was sold by her friendly attitude and outgoing nature. Home she went; initial reports were golden – everything was going swimmingly. Literally.

Seems that very quickly after getting settled into the home, Sturgeon made it clear that she wanted to get outside. While we do require all of our adopted cats to be indoors only, we have had certain cats over the years that have proven to be incredibly difficult to keep inside. We once had a cat at the Center who would literally hang from the window screens yelling at the top of his lungs, wanting to get outside. Remember Kipper and Mama Thompson? Some of the cats were really difficult to keep in. Therefore, we did understand that there were occasions where a cat, who was determined enough, was going to sneak out. And sneak out Sturgeon did; every time the owner opened her front door, which, fortunately, faced a lovely ten-acre spread, Sturgeon would dash out the door. But that wasn't all of it. Once outside, she would trot down the garden path, make her way directly to the fish pond, watch for a minute, and then leap in and paddle around.

Sturgeon loved it - I'm not sure what those Koi thought, however!

Koda

Not every cat was quite as obvious as Sturgeon in their desire to escape. One of my favorite cats ever, Koda, had been waiting patiently for an adopter for over two years. His situation was a puzzling one. He came from a loving home where he had lived since kittenhood. Another Owner Give-up situation where an infant arrived on the scene and was allergic to the point of hospital visits, Koda had to be rehomed. He went first to a Foster where he waited six weeks (our average stay in Rescue), then went to a new home, only to be returned after he bit his new owner on several different occasions. After another stint with the same Foster (he bit her too), we transferred him to the Center where, as of this writing, he continues to wait for his furever home.

Now Koda is, without a doubt, a tough cat to adopt out. The biting thing continues, appearing to be either a jealous reaction to other cats getting attention or a cry for attention when he is being ignored by whatever person is close by. We determined early on that he needed to be the only cat in the home, which always makes it more difficult to find an adopter, as so many people believe that "more is better." He is, at this point, ten years of age plus he has some spinal stenosis issues, so is very gimpy. His age, plus the pain meds he takes, puts him in the category of "medically involved," another significant deterrent to being adopted. The biggest negative, however, is that after living with so many other cats for so long at the Center, he has become not only a bit of a bully, but a sprayer. While this behavior didn't manifest itself early on, sometimes the Rescue environment actually breaks these cats, bringing out bad habits that weren't previously in existence. This is one such case. While we firmly believe that in the right home situation all of his negative behaviors wouldn't continue, when these cats are listed with so many issues in a shelter or rescue (and we always believe in telling the truth, the whole truth, and nothing but the truth), it makes it extra hard to find an adopter who is willing to give them a chance.

Earning the dubious distinction of the longest cat we've ever had at the Center waiting to be adopted, Koda decided to take matters into his own paws.

Introducing Pearl. While not a clone by any means, there were some similarities. They are both seal points, they are both about the same size, they both have a similar type of fur of the thicker variety. She, too, had been waiting for an adopter, but she had been chosen and her adopter, who lived in North Carolina, was on her way to pick her up. Being internet-based, the majority of our adopters don't get the opportunity to meet the cat first and to see the environment the cat is currently in, so it's always wonderful if they can. Pearl's adopter loved to drive, so despite the five-hour drive in each direction, she was eager to come to pick Pearl up. She planned to arrive mid-afternoon on a Wednesday.

At the time, Wednesday was my vet visit day – the day I gathered up whatever cats in the Center needed a vet visit and headed out. A twenty-minute drive in each direction, this meant I was gone anywhere from an hour to two, depending on how many cats I had and what needed to be done.

Darrell was left in charge of meeting with Pearl's adopter, collecting the adoption agreement, and sending Pearl off on her trip home. The carrier was all set up, the take-home bag packed.

Returning from the vet late that afternoon, I unloaded the cats at the Center and then went over to the house. Everything had gone without a hitch, reported Darrell; the adopter was super nice, and Pearl had walked right into the carrier when he opened the carrier door. We were always amazed at how each cat somehow knew that the carrier was their ticket home. They would always (well, okay, not all of them, but many of them) be front and center and ready to be loaded into the carrier when the time came. One major exception was, of course, the Wednesday afternoon vet visits, as you can well imagine. No one was front and center for those trips.

Anyway, it was an hour or so later when I headed over to the Center to do the evening feeding. As I walked into Group Living, who should come prancing over, looking for dinner, but Pearl.

OH NO!

At this point, I realized that the adopter had taken the wrong cat. But which cat did she have? Yup, you guessed it, she had the one and only troubled Koda cat. A cat who, in the wrong situation, was bound to bite, spray, and generally cause a lot of mayhem.

I rushed over to the house to tell Darrell the

bad news. He was confident that Pearl had walked into the carrier. One of the advantages of having cameras in the Center – we are able to get online and review the camera footage, and so we did just that. Sure enough, there was Pearl, eagerly getting in the carrier. Darrell and the adopter were talking away. Darrell handed the adopter the adoption agreement, which she signed, giving it back to Darrell. He turned around to make a copy. And there was Koda, approaching the carrier, glaring at Pearl (she quickly exited the carrier), and elbowing his way into the carrier where he plopped down, looking very pleased with himself. Darrell turned back to the adopter, handed her a copy of the agreement, and leaned down to close the carrier door. Perfect, except the wrong cat!

Well, it's dinner time on Wednesday, and we needed to fix the situation quickly. We were certainly not going to ask the adopter to turn around and drive back here, so we called the adopter, explained what happened, and asked her to put Koda in a room by himself, leaving him in his carrier (no touching). We packed up Pearl and got into the car, heading to North Carolina.

Fast forward eight hours; it's about 2am by the time we got home. To compensate poor Koda, who thought he had a "get out of jail free" card, he rode the five hours back on my lap, during which time he did nothing but purr. Yes, this was completely against all of our transport rules (cats must stay in the carrier), but we felt it was the least we could offer him. Returning to the Center, he took one look around him and let out a huge hiss. And yes, he continues to try to make his great escape with every other carrier that is readied for transport, but we are now wise to his trick!

Now, this was not the only time that we managed to "lose" a cat. Peanut (aptly named) was a small, six-pound chocolate point male who came from a hoarding situation; we had taken about seven out of the thirty cats that were in that home. He was doing fairly well over at the Center, well adjusted in Group Living – superbly cat-oriented, as many of the hoarder cats often were. Shyer with humans, he did fine if there was just one or two of us over there, but would often hide if it got too noisy.

We found a fantastic adopter for him – she had one other cat, a very quiet home, and a basket full of patience. She was close enough to pick him up from the Center, so we set an appointment for her to visit, and I got his carrier and his take-home bag ready. At the time there were twenty or so cats downstairs. The cages were left open so the cats could enter and exit as they pleased, and there was climbing apparatus galore – basically many, many places to hide. This, we found, was the best way to manage a large group living situation without a lot of squabbles – have plenty of spaces (vertical as well as floor level) to allow the cats to spread out as far as they wanted to within the confines of the room.

The adopter arrived, and as typically happens,

we spent the first ten to fifteen minutes with the usual "meet and greet." Those cats that had Adoption 101 down pat were front and center, begging for attention. Those that were not so sure were hanging on the sidelines watching how it was done, and those that were sulking, moody or plain not interested, were lounging somewhere ignoring us. As I was introducing each cat, I was keeping my eye out for Peanut as, of course, he was the one she planned to take home. We moved through the room, and as each introduction was completed, I was getting just a bit more concerned, for Peanut was nowhere to be found. All of the usual hiding places were empty.

By now we had met all of the cats both milling around and hiding, and the adopter was looking at me expectantly, ready to meet Peanut. Now, the search began in earnest. Section by section of the room we checked - behind the fridge, inside the cabinets, on top of the shelves. There was *no* Peanut to be found, not anywhere. My mind recalled a similar situation a few years earlier when an adopter had come to visit a cat, and we couldn't find the cat. It turned out that as the adopter and her somewhat overweight mother were coming through the front door, the cat in question exited the door, and it was only after spending quite some time searching that I happened to glance out the window and see the cat happily chewing on a blade of grass. Fortunately, we were able to catch that cat, and the next day, we installed a double door system so that wouldn't happen again. Because of the double door system (only one door gets opened at a time), I was confident Peanut was still in the building. That didn't help us, however, when after about two hours of Darrell and I searching high and low, we had to, with extremely red faces, admit defeat and apologize profusely to the adopter that somehow we had lost *her* cat.

Since that time, we've had cats who could open cabinets and hunker down behind the cans of cat food. We had one who pulled a "Squirrel" on us and got inside a drawer; we even had a cat jump out of the refrigerator one time when we opened it after a volunteer inadvertently closed her in. But Peanut took the cake – he was, by far, the master Houdini.

Peanut did eventually go home. We found him, later that evening, inside a near-empty Kleenex box on a very high shelf in the bathroom!

WE'RE EXPERIENCING TECHNICAL DIFFICULTIES

There are many benefits to having a techno-wizard for a husband (#2 for those keeping score), particularly when it comes to having a small animal shelter on your private property. In the early days, despite the fact that one passes right by the front of the house when driving up to the Center, there would be times when I might be doing a load of laundry, or out back gardening, or maybe just focused while talking on the phone – and I would not see the car come in the driveway. An hour or so later, I'd wander over to the Center, only to find some family sitting on the floor, playing with the cats. Yes, the Center is located on what is clearly private property – there's nothing commercial about it. No, it would not be considered reasonable to just walk into someone's garage and make yourself at home. Maybe they knocked, and the cats said to come in. I guess we'll never know.

Well, the unexpected intruder situation could be fairly easily fixed. Darrell installed an alarm that went off every time someone drove in the driveway, as well as a punch code lock on the Center door. Additionally, every time that door was opened, an announcement came on in the house. At least now, if I'm upstairs in my PJ's, I know I need to hastily get dressed and make my way next door to greet whoever has come by. Other automation he installed allows us to monitor the property from afar so that rather than being on the property 24/7, we can regulate the temperature in each section of the Center, we can turn lights on and off, we can speak to someone who is there, and, of course, we can watch what's going on. Living in a very rural part of Virginia, winters could be full of downed trees, etc., so we have alarms that sound (and email us) if the electricity goes off and backup generators that come on (one of the best things ever). It only took one time with no heat in a cement-floored garage (albeit well insulated) with thirty cats in that space, to realize that moving all of those cats into heated cars was not going to happen easily. And now, of course, we even have Alexa and all her personalities and abilities. (While I've made peace with the other Siri, Alexa and I are still working out our differences.)

But it is, without a doubt, the cameras that provide the most entertainment.

There are numerous cameras. We have one in the Isolation Room, which is great because it became easy to determine if the cat that had just arrived and was hunkered down behind the litterbox was truly terrified, or was just being a drama puss. (If it was a blue point, most likely the latter.) Many times, the minute you left the building, the cat would sit up, look around, check out the food, and act reasonably normal – until, of course, they heard the door open again. There is a camera in the upstairs of the Center so we can observe the four to eight cats we keep up there (a quieter area for the shyer cats who aren't yet ready to interact in the Group Living environment). There are two cameras in Group Living, allowing us to keep an eye on all of the cats downstairs, making sure one isn't picking on another.

Additionally, in watching the group interaction from afar, we can see which cats get along with other cats, as well as identify more about their personalities to share with adopters. There is another camera outside, sometimes pointed at the garden, sometimes aiming down the driveway at the entrance to the property. And finally, there is the one showcasing the fantastic view of the Blue Ridge Mountains that we are fortunate to have off our front deck.

Of all the funny camera experiences, however, nothing quite compares to the episode in the bedroom. The camera that showcases the gorgeous view of the mountains? While that camera is now secured on the outside corner of our house, at the time, Darrell had it perched temporarily on the window sill of the dormer in our bedroom. (This already sounds like a bad idea, right?)

It was late one evening, and I had gone to bed before Darrell – it's summertime, and let's just say I was not dressed in full flannel pajamas. Okay, okay, I boasted that we always tell the truth, so here it is, I was waltzing around buck-naked. As I entered the bedroom, my nose told me that maybe the cats' pan (located in a library-type room adjacent to the master bedroom) needed cleaning – something definitely smelled pretty funky. I checked the pan, gave it a scoop, yet that odd smell still seemed to be permeating the bedroom. Unable to find anything, I got into bed and settled under the covers. Slipping my hand under my pillow, and ACCCCKKK. Something really awful was under there – a little furry, a little bony – no idea what it was. Lifting the pillow to take a look, there, to my horror, was a desiccated, quite ancient, mummified mouse. And sitting not three feet away from me, watching every move with a big smile on her face, was our seal point gal, Britainy, looking incredibly pleased with herself.

Britainy

Now as a child in central New York, we lived in quite rustic conditions in a very countrified cabin that was not well insulated. Much of the time we relied on the living room fireplace for heat, and the bedrooms were *cold*, so I'd snuggle way down in bed, topped with heaps of blankets. One of my worst memories ever was waking up in the middle of the night to find one of our cats sitting on my chest, holding a mouse in his mouth. Of course, I let out a whopper of scream, at which point the cat dropped the still squirming critter in the bed and took off. I never got over that experience, and seeing this mummified mouse brought back all of that horror, plus some. I ricocheted off the bed and flew around the room, screaming like a banshee chicken. The blankets came off the bed, the bedside light was knocked over, the cats were scrambling in every direction, and I was about as traumatized as I could be. Darrell came racing up the stairs to my rescue - he got the bed stripped, and the sheets replaced, and finally, after a good five minutes, I managed to calm down and get back into bed. What an awful experience, one that I will *never* forget!

It was a good thirty minutes later, my heartbeat having finally returned to normal speed, when I looked over by the window and noticed that the camera was no longer perched on that bedroom window sill. And where was it? At the end of the bed, on the floor pointing towards the center of the room – right where I had been doing the Dead Mouse Dance. There it sat, broadcasting live to the world. While no one ever commented to either of us about those five minutes, I had to wonder what kind of show I put on for some unsuspecting cat lover! (Our donations did not skyrocket, so maybe no one was impressed by my middle-aged body? And yes, there probably is a website, someplace, where you can see naked ladies scooping litterboxes. I promise it won't be me though.) You can be assured, after that episode, I demanded the camera be permanently removed from the bedroom!

That experience was by far the most intimate I ever got with any of our cat-loving public, but there were several other times that sharing one's personal environment with the general public was a challenge. I am an avid flower gardener and surrounding the house and the Center, as well as in the area that stretches between the two, I designed umpteen different flower beds. In one area, measuring perhaps ten foot by ten foot, we had laid a square of bricks, and as one of our fundraisers, people could purchase a brick to either honor or memorialize a cat (or a person). We would have the brick engraved with the cat's name and date, and it would be laid in what came to be known as the Memorial Garden. Over the years, many of the donors would visit, find their brick, and sit on the bench in the shade, enjoying the country atmosphere. Surrounding the square of bricks were the various flower beds, as well as a small waterfall culminating in a fish pond that Darrell designed. It was a lovely, spiritual and peaceful place.

I take great pride in the garden – working in it is

not only a good stress reliever for me, but I love the designing and organizing of the plants into various sections. Every few years, I order several tons of mulch, and I spend countless hours distributing it to the different flower beds, tucking everything in nice and neatly. For someone who grew up in a very volatile home environment, this gives me a real feeling of safety, security, and comfort.

It was one such spring, and I had just finished three days of moving, wheelbarrow after wheelbarrow, all of the mulch that had been delivered. Now every few years I would try a different type and size of mulch, keeping notes as to how it looked, how long it lasted, how it affected the pH of the soil, and so forth. And every time that the dump truck arrives with the three tons of mulch, I gulp at the enormous amount of work I have just committed to. Good exercise though, and well worth it in the end. That particular year I had gone with a large nugget dark brown pine mulch, and although one of the more expensive years for mulch, it really looked great – very professional. I was really pleased with the outcome.

About two days after I had finished with the mulch project (my back was killing me), I got a phone call from one of our very long-term volunteers. They were retiring to Texas, and, in downsizing their belongings, they asked permission to bring the ashes of their previous cats to bury in the Memorial Garden. Not a problem. This was not such an unusual request; we actually had quite a few feline and canine bodies and/or ashes already buried on the property. Darrell always joked that one day, well in the future, paleontologists would be digging on our property and wonder what strange cult of cat worshippers had lived here. It was perfectly fine, I told those volunteers, to bring the ashes and bury them.

And so they did. No, not just the ashes of a few cats, but the ashes of many. I lost count after the tenth ceramic container was opened and the ashes dispersed. And yes, they were scattered. Before I could say anything, both husband and wife were opening container after container and sprinkling ashes everywhere, as if salting the garden. Ashes, dark gray ashes, now covered all of that lovely brown mulch. Sure, the next rain would soak them into the mulch and likely provide great nitrogen for the plants. But at the time, all I could do was stare in disbelief as my *Better Homes and Gardens* layout was covered in cat ashes.

Of course, I never said anything, (and if you are reading this, it's okay). I understood this was an emotional time for them, and in the big scheme of things, this was small. As a matter of fact, after they left, I went into the shed and pulled out someone's cat ashes that had arrived in the mail. No, I didn't know the person; the ashes came with a note asking me to please keep the ashes safely, and added those to the rest.

IT'S ALL ABOUT THE CATS – OR IS IT?

As you may remember, I went from the profession of teaching, dealing with not only the kids, but also the parents, to cat rescue - thinking, somewhat mistakenly, that it would be mostly about the cats. After all the years of doing this, I now know that's not true. The cats, of course, came from a wide variety of backgrounds and situations, and when comparing cat personalities, even though we could make generalizations, no two cats were ever the same. It goes without saying that this applies to people too. What made Rescue so challenging was the constant turn of that roulette wheel as we worked to match the cats to the people.

While we loved having visitors (and would encourage them to join our Saturday pot luck lunches with the Kennel Crew if they came on that day), I would always cringe a little bit when a family with younger children came to visit. Not that I don't love children, with a background in teaching, of course I do, but since rescue cats typically come from backgrounds of abandonment and often of abuse, many of them just aren't childproof. Add into that the fact that the Center typically houses the longer term (as in more behaviorally challenged) cats, and there is always a bit of a safety concern when I see a family approaching with little people excitedly jumping up and down.

One such family that came to visit comes to mind. They were approved to adopt, having called in advance to set up an appointment (pat on the head for that). We were a bit worried, however, about being able to find the perfect match for this particular home, as they had a ten-year-old autistic son whose behavior included loud noises and lots of energetic activity. We knew that given the background of most of our cats, many of them were likely to be taken aback. In preparation, we cleared the downstairs of the extremely timid cats that would obviously be overwhelmed by any loud noises, hoping for the best with the rest of them.

Sure enough, as the whirlwind of fast-paced running and vocalizations began, cats sped off in every direction, disappearing under cage banks and into hidey beds and cat condos. There wasn't a cat to be found - that is, except PowPow.

PowPow was a young, energetic, female flame from a public shelter; she had been turned in by her family due to her "inability to get along" with others. A guest at the Center for about four weeks, I was worried about finding her the type of home she seemed to need. She was very high energy, so she needed an active household; she would never do in a sedate living environment. She didn't play well with other cats, misreading their body language and getting all worked up if they got too close to her personal space. Unfortunately, she didn't appear to be all that keen on people either – while she wasn't aggressive in any way shape or form, she was somewhat aloof, and responded with the "cold shoulder" when most people tried to interact with her. She had several potential adopters visit her to date, but she made it abundantly clear that she didn't like any of them, absolutely refusing to even give them the time of day.

Seated atop a cat tree when the family entered the room, PowPow watched with interest as the boy twirled around in circles, waving his arms and whooping. She wasn't frightened, she wasn't taken aback, she just calmly sat there, observing. After about a minute or so of consideration, PowPow jumped down from her perch and walked towards this boy with interest.

It was the darndest thing. As the boy ran around, she trotted behind him, right on his heels. As he turned in circles, she stopped and watched, not more than a foot away, a grin on her face. When he moved, she moved, almost as if in sync. And when he stopped, she rubbed up against him.

As his energy gave out, he sank to the floor, wrapping his arms around his knees and curling up on himself. And what did PowPow do? She went right up to him, nudged his arms aside, and parked herself in his lap. It was truly one of the most amazing things we had ever seen. Both his parents, as well as Darrell and myself, were dumbstruck. PowPow had clearly made up her mind and chosen her adopter. And yes, of course she went home, and they were best buds.

For PowPow, the decision was obvious; she made it purrfectly clear to all of us that it was a match made in heaven, as they say. Here I had been worried that no cat would match with the situation at hand, and yet we saw the most perfect match happen right before our very eyes. It really was something extraordinary to witness.

On the other end of the spectrum, however, was a visit by an adopter where no amount of convincing, by any of a large number of amazing cats, could seal an adoption.

The inability to make up one's mind can be understandable when faced with a litter of adorable kittens, or even webpage after webpage of great looking cats to choose from. We understand that. And in our business, we know that spending a lot of time, and then some, with the various adopters as they interact with the various cats, is part of the process. After all, we don't want anyone making a decision in haste, we had concerns in the past when someone walked in and immediately made a comment such as "this one will be fine." We once had an adopter choose a cat the moment she walked in the door, based on the cat's coloring matching her sofa. Yes, people really do say this; it's okay, the match actually ended up being a good one, both color-wise and personality-wise. A careful evaluation of all the pros and cons of each cat before making a decision is always ideal. Some adopters, however, took this to the extreme.

Being internet-based, and having the Meezer Express set up to help with the transport of the cat from foster home to permanent home, the majority of our applicants would adopt off of the website. MOMS offered an interactive system where they looked at pictures, watched videos, read detailed write-ups and reviewed medical records, and then talked on the phone to the foster parent. Applicants could enter their zip code on the website, and the system would bring up the selection of cats within their geographic (transport) region. Geographic regions were determined by where we had volunteer transport assistance; most cats could travel up to ten hours away from the foster home. This meant that a foster cat in Virginia might find an adopter in Connecticut, and the Meezer Express would work as a relay team to get the cat home.

In order to consider the various cats within their transport region, applicants clicked above the cat's picture on the website. This sent an email to the foster parent who then sent a write up about the cat to the applicant. Many of the more popular cats would hold long interest lists (or dance cards as I referred to them). The Fosters would work with the first person at the top of the list (i.e., that applicant who asked first) to determine if the cat was a match; if so, that was great, and an adoption would occur. If not, that person first in line would be bypassed, and the Foster would move down the list to the next applicant in line.

This particular applicant (a single woman in her thirties) had been driving the Fosters absolutely crazy. She had clicked on numerous cats: males and females, young and old, every color that we had available. She had moved to the top of the dance card on a number of them but just was not able to make a decision. This held up the adoption process for not only the cats, but for many other applicants who were behind her on the list for the different cats that she was considering. After going back and forth with her and realizing that she just couldn't pull the trigger, we suggested (insisted) that we bypass her for all the cats whose list she was on, and that she set up an appointment to visit the Center. Here, she could interact with a variety of cats at one time. Surely, face-to-face with a lot of wonderful Siamese, and with me standing there with her to discuss all the plusses and minuses of each cat, she'd be able to decide.

We set up an appointment. It was mid-summer, and the choices were plenty – we must have had twenty-five different cats in Group Living at the time. There were males and females in every point color there is. There were young cats and old cats, friendly cats, and fraidy cats. Some were purebred looking, some not so much. At first, patiently, and then later on, not quite so patiently, we discussed each cat to the nth degree, trying to help her decide via detailed explanations and leading questions. By 7pm that evening (yes, eight hours into her visit) we were spent, and she was no closer to making a decision than she had been when she arrived. Not one to give up her pursuit of perfection, however, she asked if she could come back the following day, and we hesitatingly agreed.

The next day unraveled just like the first, an enormous amount of time and discussion but no decision. By the time 5pm rolled around, both Darrell and I were at our wit's end. It was time to choose or time to leave, but definitely time to do something. While I hated to admit it, at this point we really didn't care what cat she took – we were just over the entire situation. We practically jumped for joy when she finally made a decision, choosing one of the many cats who buddied up to her in those two days of visiting.

Wishing her well, we couldn't send her off much faster than we did. Wooeey, did we feel we had earned that adoption fee!

But wait - why was she stopped, parked, at the end of the driveway, for one minute, three minutes, five minutes. Really? Please don't tell us. Maybe we could both escape out the back door and disappear. We could feign death, something, anything not to have to have this continue any longer. No such luck. Sure enough, there was her car, reversing down the driveway. Back in she walked to the Center, cat carrier in hand. She just wasn't sure and wanted to back out of the adoption.

Oh my. We sent the adopter on her way, no cat in hand, thinking that perhaps a Beanie Baby might be better suited. One had to wonder what she did for a living – hopefully nothing that required much in the way of decision making!

While that lady took the cake for the fastest return ever, we have had some other mind-boggling ones. Like everything else in our program, our protocols have improved considerably over the years, thanks to our incredible Lead Interviewers. Five years or so into Siamese Rescue, we had developed an amazing matchmaking process. We found that by the Interviewers gathering as much information about the applicant and their family, and the Fosters gathering as much information about the cat, and then both of them documenting all of this where it could be reviewed and analyzed by the parties directly involved, we'd get a solid match. And most of the time, we did.

Every once in a while an applicant will return a cat for some of the strangest reasons, sometimes even within a day or two. One lady decided she would rather be a dog person – such a surprising thing to say after she had gone to all the trouble and expense of getting a cat and all the supplies. Another couple complained that their new kittens were keeping too active. There were several adopters who expected the new cat to rush with open paws towards the existing cat (sorry, this rarely happens). We once had an applicant pick up a cat from a foster home, drive out the driveway, hear a sneeze, and turn around and return the cat because she felt it was deathly ill (the cat was fine, it was probably a little pollen). For all the wild and crazy returns, while we would scratch our heads in amazement, we always figured it was better for the cat as in the end, we found a much better match for them.

I think the scariest return situation we ever had, however, was an adoption of a lovely, young, energetic male cat that a family had adopted as a birthday gift for their young son. The family lived in an area that was hard to access and one in which we didn't have much in the way of volunteer coverage. They went through the screening process, but no matter how careful one is, sometimes someone slips through the cracks. This was a young couple: the father worked in law enforcement, the mother was a homemaker, and they had just the one son, no other pets. They were anxious to adopt in time for the birthday and sailed through the application process. Knowing that the cat was being chosen as a companion for their son, we suggested a wonderful male seal point who was well adjusted, healthy, loving, and playful – a perfect, childproof cat.

The cat had been in the home for about a week and the boy's birthday party had been held. The phone rang at 9pm one night; typically we wouldn't pick up the phone this late, but recognizing the adopter's name on the caller ID, we did thank goodness. It was the husband, and he was ranting and raving like there was no end in sight. Apparently the cat, when frightened at the party, had urinated on the pile of birthday presents. The father was so angry that he told us if we weren't there to pick up the cat in half an hour, he was going to take it outside and shoot it. I'm not kidding. And all of this in an area that is not easily accessible and is many hours drive away.

PowPow

Thinking fast, we managed to find a local vet who, once he heard the story, agreed to reopen his office and accept the cat to board overnight. One has to wonder if this guy's reputation preceded him. We convinced the father to drop off the cat at the vet's office, and the following day, found a volunteer willing to go get this cat and return it to the Foster. Fortunately unaffected, the cat went on to be placed in a great home, and all was well. Needless to say, that applicant was marked as disapproved!

YOU ARE AMAZING, DAHLING!

There is so much that has gone into the running of this organization, from the Crafters making catnip pillows and toys for the cats, to the Transporters who are driving the cats, and everyone else in between. It would have been impossible to have done this without our volunteers and supporters, there is no doubt. They are the ones who have given us the ability to make such a difference in so many lives.

The supporters helped in so many ways imaginable. There were the regular donors: those who found us in year one and continued to support us either every month or every year thereafter. There were the gifts from those who made a one-time donation, to those who remembered us in their wills, allowing us to make larger purchases, as well as the ability to help in other ways. And there was the constant flow of goodies: when we would post our Amazon Wish List online, the UPS man would comment that it was like Christmas, once even delivering twenty-five boxes of Wish List items in one day.

Of course, not everything that arrived in the mail is what we expected. We have a couple of dedicated supporters who must travel the world (perhaps via the internet) buying up every kind of Siamese-related item you can imagine – from stuffed animals to porcelain figurines to slippers. Boxes of these items would arrive every so often and were used for our auctions and raffles at Siamese Cat Rescue events. Some of the time we knew the person responsible for sending the gifts, other times we had no idea who it was. Either way, we were always appreciative and worked hard to be sure to reach out with a thank you, but several times we were on the receiving end, and have felt truly helpless.

One such situation was a gentleman in New York who, over the years, sent us small items here and there, always enclosing a picture and a story about his cat. Clearly very lonely, it was apparent that his Siamese, whom he stated was his only friend, provided him with the thread that tethered him to this world. Without appearing to have much of a support system, his letters got sadder and sadder as time went on and as his cat aged up. We responded to each note, sending our thank you with a Siamese cat calendar or sometimes a toy for his cat. One day, however, a box arrived in the mail – and to my horror, I discovered it was his cat's ashes. With it was a note asking me to hold these for a short while, that his ashes would follow. This was not someone we knew, merely someone who found us over the internet, so we had limited contact information. After a bit of research, we were able to track down an area minister who had previously counseled this gentleman, and alerted him to what sounded to us like a possible end-of-life note. We never did hear back, never did receive any additional ashes, and after a few years, added his cat's ashes to the others that were sprinkled in our Memorial Garden.

A similar situation occurred when one of our early volunteer Transporters had fallen on hard times. She sent me a letter, letting me know that she was being evicted and that she was putting all her worldly goods into her car and leaving the Rescue both her car and the goods. Another worrisome situation, as again this sounded like a plea for help. After spending several hours on the phone alerting various suicide intervention agencies (all of whom kept focusing on how I felt, saying they couldn't do anything at all unless she called), it occurred to us to contact the emergency contact she had listed on her volunteer application – a brother – and let him know about the note and our concerns.

A few weeks later, her brother called. Sadly, she had followed through, and he was boxing up the belongings and sending them along to us (to include a collection of antique dolls which we were able to sell on eBay and raise quite a bit of money).

The entire experience, however, was upsetting – and certainly not something one thinks one would encounter in the running of a cat rescue. Once again, it was apparent how the intricate ties between cats and people affect so many.

Finally, there are those things that the amazing volunteers gave us. The majority of these things were fantastic – chocolate cake, homemade jams, little Siamese mementos. There were gifts for the garden, a quilt for the wall, an embroidered wall hanging, and framed photographs to display at the Center. One-of-a-kind things, often handmade, that meant so very much.

And then there's The Serval.

It was at Spring Training one year – our annual gathering of a hundred or so of our volunteers who descended on the Mother Ship (aka the Center) to share in feline fun and training for the Rescue. This was a huge event and something that we both planned for and looked forward to all year long. We rented an enormous tent and fed, entertained and trained the volunteers for two solid days. Many of the vets we worked with would come and share their expertise and experience via various workshops that covered everything from diabetes in cats to behavior management in multi-cat households. There were auctions and raffles; we played all sorts of games: litterbox scooping and cat carrier races and scavenger hunts. It was an opportunity for volunteers from the far reaches of our internet-based program to get together and physically meet and greet people they primarily interacted with by email. Lots and lots of fun.

While each year we did something slightly different, we always gave out thank you gifts and awards on Saturday evening. The award presentations would consist of both recognitions for volunteer service, as well as booby prizes. Capitalizing on the Chicken Dance that soulmate and mascot Alfonso P. Wallabee had done as he raced in circles around the kitchen island, we awarded chicken hats to those who were involved with the "Page One" cats. (On the website we display cats by date, so the Page One cats are the cats who have been in the program the longest.) Any volunteer who had been involved during that year with the adoption of a Page One cat (Evaluator or Foster of the cat, Interviewer of the applicant who adopted the cat, or Transporter who helped transport the cat) got the dubious honor of being called up, asked to don a chicken hat, and then participate in the Chicken Dance. It became a hysterically silly tradition that volunteers both wanted to be, and

dreaded being, a part of. And yes, I got to lead it each year.

This particular year, after the awards had been presented and the Chicken Dance was completed, one of our volunteers (you know who you are) held up his hand to call everyone to attention. Before everyone dispersed, he had a special gift he wanted to present to me as Director. Handing me an enormous box, I dutifully started unwrapping – layer after layer of packing materials – and underneath it all, I found something fuzzy. No, not another desiccated mouse. Pulling it out, it was a taxidermy Serval.

Now don't get me wrong, this is a lovely gentleman who volunteered in several different capacities and deeply loved the cats. He had, on numerous occasions, gone above and beyond the call of normal volunteer work, visiting adopters' homes after the fact to help them with their cats, inviting potential adopters for a meal when considering a cat – a very kind and generous person. That having been said, however, the receipt of one very dead animal as a gift, and a cat no less, required incredible facial expression control on my part. (I was told I managed quite well, despite the obvious shock I felt upon realizing what it was.)

While I know one is not supposed to look a gift horse in the mouth, or in this case, a Serval, I did very gently decline the gift and ask that he take it back home with him.

THE FINAL CHAPTER?

While I have always loved animals, I "fell" into Animal Rescue. While I knew a little something about cats, I didn't know much about running a business, let alone a non-profit. What I thought would be helping just a few cats quickly evolved into a full-time passion. And I certainly never realized how much people-time would be involved.

Once I got started, I thought I'd be spending most of my time involved with the cats, never realizing there was so much more to Rescue than the animals. While I had no idea how emotional and often times frustrating Rescue would be, I also had no understanding of how rewarding life would become. In a world where there is so much sadness, it has been wonderful to be able to fill so many empty buckets – my own, as well as others.

The team experience was a new one for me. Growing up, there were never that many people I enjoyed being around. I felt ostracized in high school. I didn't fit the social strata in college. Even early on as a mother, I felt fairly isolated in the community. Rescue introduced me to a new "breed" of people. People who agreed to step up in every way imaginable to help. So many people coming together for the good of so many cats. It boggles my mind.

The quality of the program has been in direct correlation to the quality of our volunteers. We were a tough group to volunteer for as we set high expectations early on, established consequences for various behaviors and actions, and were, at times, quite tough on the volunteers. They went through a solid screening process (references and interview, even if they were going to make cat toys for our group); Fosters, Interviewers, and Evaluators committed to an in-depth training program (videos, home visits, training tapes, and multiple interviews). We 'hired and fired' as if we had employees. We certainly made mistakes, just like we did in the rest of the program, as we learned to oversee close to 3,000 volunteers. What we ended up with, however, was a group of volunteers who would go to the ends of the earth, not only for the cats and the adopters but for each other. Driving to pick up an applicant or adopter whose car had broken down. Sending cat food and supplies to someone who was struggling financially. Taking up a collection to pay the landlord deposit so that a lonely, elderly man could have a cat in his apartment. Showing up at an adopter's house, late at night, shovel in hand, to bury their cat.

Put all of these fantastic people together – not only our volunteers, but our supporters and our adopters, and what do you get? You get the paychecks of Rescue. The warm glow that fills your soul when an elderly lady finds a new best friend. The ear-to-ear smile on the young girl's face when her new cat loves being pushed around in the baby carriage. The reassurance you see on the face of the elderly man entering a nursing facility when he knows his cat will be cared for. And, of course, the purrs and headbutts and soulful appreciation emanating from the eyes of cats like Mr. Bibbles. Rescue helped me find my reason for being.

Nothing stays the same over time, however. This can be a good thing, as we learn from the past and improve our thoughts and actions. It can also be a sad thing, as both the needs and the parameters inevitably change.

In the field of Animal Rescue, there have been significant improvements in many areas. There are way more spay/neuter programs out there, and while there is no doubt that many rural areas still struggle, great efforts have been made to stem the overpopulation problem by curbing some of the unwanted animal pregnancies. Many of the urban animal shelters and SPCAs have been able to build fantastic shelter facilities, and with such, really focus on matchmaking and adoptions – a real help to the no-kill movement. While we still have a long way to go, and there will always be animals in need of help, the requests for assistance from the large shelters we have worked with over the years has decreased significantly. This is a great thing.

As Darrell and I have aged up, so have our volunteers. The majority of our volunteers were with us for years - we have shared births and deaths, graduations and retirements, illnesses and recoveries. Finding new volunteers, however, has always been difficult. As an organization, our volunteer participation has decreased over time. Coupled with some of the changes in Animal Rescue, we see a shift in our focus. As we head into the future, Siamese Cat Rescue will concentrate more on supporting, mentoring, and networking, and be a bit less hands-on than we've been in the past.

In looking back over the years, we marvel at how we were so very fortunate to find our niche and to fill it so successfully. We have grown both with and through Siamese Rescue, and are very thankful for all the wonderful people and the great cats we have met as we made this colorful journey.

I look forward to the next chapter.